revelation of Revelation

I0142275

AN URGENT MESSAGE FOR THE CHURCH

VOLUME 3
THE SEVEN SEALS OF REVELATION

*The First Narrative
of
Revelation*

Rev 4:1-11:18

The Naked Apostles
Phil and Colleen Livingston

Published by: The Naked Apostles

WAUCONDA, IL

Phil and Colleen Livingston/The Naked Apostles
304 Barrington Road
Wauconda, IL 60084
www.nakedapostles.org
email: info@nakedapostles.org

Ordering Information:
Quantity sales. Special discounts are available on quantity purchases by corporations, associations, and others. For details, contact via email or the address above.

revelation of Revelation, *An Urgent Message for the Church* Volume 3: The Seven Seals of Revelation/The Naked Apostles, Phil and Colleen Livingston. 2.2
ISBN 978-0-9960102-6-9

Table of Contents

Chapter 1: Introduction to the Visions Spoken to John 1

Chapter 2: The Throne in Heaven.. 11

Chapter 3: The Scroll and the Lamb 19

Chapter 4: The First Four Seals 39

Chapter 5: The Fifth Seal.. 55

Chapter 6: The Sixth Seal 61

Chapter 7: The Seventh Seal 85

Chapter 8: The Seven Trumpets of the Seventh Seal........................... 91

Bibliography... 143

About the Authors 145

Dedicated to the 144,000, the first fruits of Jesus' redeeming work. May their sacrifice be remembered and their integrity followed.

He who overcomes will inherit these things, and I will be his God and he will be My son.

— Revelation 21:7 New American Standard Bible

Volume 1

Introduction to Revelation

Volume 2

The Seven Letters of Revelation
1:1-3:22

Volume 3

The Seven Seals of Revelation
The first narrative of the vision
4:1-11:18

Volume 4

The Main Characters of Revelation
The second narrative of the vision
11:19-16:21

Volume 5

The Fall of Babylon and the Church Corrupt
The third narrative of the vision
17:1-21:8

Volume 6

The New Jerusalem
The fourth narrative of the vision
21:9-22:21

CHAPTER 1

Introduction to the Visions Spoken to John

R evelation is a series of visions. To interpret them here are a few important factors which are required:

- Understanding how these visions are outlined.
- How they relate to each other.
- Discovering the scope and timelines of the visions.
- Then possessing the proper points of reference on the timelines that the different elements represent.
- Discovering a singular context which brings continuity to, not only the visions of Revelation, but all Biblical prophecy without causing one to contradict the other.
- Then, finding a meaning of what each element in the visions represent, a meaning which supports a single context without skewing it or the timeline. If the meaning assigned to the elements in a vision do not support a singular context or skews it, that indicates either the context is wrong or the meaning assigned to the elements are wrong. There are no random or extra parts when it comes to visions given by God.

All these factors are the keys to interpretation of a vision or dream. In the final analysis, what gives you the greatest possible affirmation that you have a proper and accurate interpretation is to possess a singular context. A context that works flawlessly with all the assigned meanings of the elements in the vision, without robbing the vision of its continuity. Have just one of these factors not fit in or support the others, then you know your interpretation is not yet accurate.

These factors along with supernatural insight and a spiritual perspective are the very things which the Lord and His angel Gabriel brought to the authors in order to release the meaning and message of the book of Revelation. After having unlocked the meaning and message of Revelation, it became clearly apparent that one cannot have true insight and understanding of the meanings of the entire Bible unless one has learned to understand the book of Revelation. Revelation is not only the key, but the missing link which unlocks and fills in the blanks of all Biblical prophecy, finally tying them all together.

First, there are the seven letters to the seven churches. In them Jesus speaks directly to His Church, together they are a singular personal letter from Him to us, they are to all the churches of all time. By doing so, He is being as true to His body in the world/His Church as He was when He was here. That is in the sense that Jesus tells us everything which He and His Father plan to do, and exactly what is in store for us.

NIV Rev 17:8 The beast, which you saw, once was, now is not, and will come up out of the Abyss and go to his destruction. The inhabitants of the earth whose names have not been written in the book of life from the creation of the world will be astonished when they see the beast, because he once was, now is not, and yet will come.

The above verse assumes the full disclosure Jesus shares with His body in the earth. When the beast is brought back from the dead this will be an event that amazes and astonishes everyone who has ever been born from the beginning of creation, living or dead. That is with the exception of His elect. Why not them? To His true body of elect, He has, does, and always will tell them everything which is to come and why.

One might say, however, that for centuries everything has been locked away right there in front of us in the Scriptures. In answer, when the Apostles walked the earth, and during the first-century, this was not so. The elect of Jesus at that time well understood all which would happen. They only lacked a sense of time it would take for these things to unfold and evolve into a global fruition. There is a reason for this phenomena that causes the contemporary church to be in the dark. And that reason was likewise revealed to us in these very letters.

NIV Rev 3:2 *Wake up! Strengthen what remains and is about to die, for I have not found your deeds complete in the sight of my God.*

NIV Rev 3:3 *Remember, therefore, what you have received and heard; obey it, and repent. But if you do not wake up, I will come like a thief, and you will not know at what time I will come to you.*

NIV Rev 3:4 *Yet you have a few people in Sardis who have not soiled their clothes. They will walk with me, dressed in white, for they are worthy.*

NIV Rev 3:5 *He who overcomes will, like them, be dressed in white. I will never blot out his name from the book of life, but will acknowledge his name before my Father and his angels.*

NIV Rev 3:6 *He who has an ear, let him hear what the Spirit says to the churches.*

Although this is spoken to the church of Sardis, it is spoken to the whole Church concerning the fifth Church age in keeping with the sevenness of the entire Church over all its history, past, present, and future. This is verified by the last line when Jesus says, "He who has an ear, let him hear <u>what the Spirit says to the churches.</u>" It does not say, what the Spirit says to Sardis.

The fifth Church age is the time period when Jesus called His elect out of the Babylonian Church of Rome through the prophetic voices of the Church reformers. That was after the fourth Church age during which He had punished her by killing her children (her followers/congregation), primarily using the Black Plague to do so.

More to the point, Jesus told all the churches from this (the fifth) Church age forward, that unless we remember (what we received from the very beginning in the first-century) the Church will not know the time He comes and will be astonished just as the rest of the world.

"Remember, therefore, what you have received and heard; obey it, and repent." In saying this Jesus is putting squarely on us to remember first-century understanding and values. In other words, we need to do whatever necessary to go back and find out that which was lost, then for us to obey it and repent.

Is this mass deception and ignorance a continuation of the same punishment that killed most of the Christian Church through the Black Plague? We only know what we know, how can we remember what we don't know, what those before us have forgotten and strayed from? Is this another case of the sins of the fathers being visited on the sons?

This "wake up" call and the ensuing consequences of not answering the call is urgent! This is eye opening information! Jesus, our Lord and Savior is saying we cannot just join the Church taking it for granted the status quo is ok, believing the established Church knows how to do "church." Jesus is saying, even if you have come out of the Roman Church of Babylon that is not enough. Jesus is actually telling us it is every individual's responsibility that we have to remember that which this generation of believers were never told, and what is not being practiced. Jesus tells us that if we do not, we will remain in ignorance.

We will remain in the dark as the rest of the world and we too will be caught unaware and astonished concerning what will happen. He and His Father are not changing their plans. This (salvation) is a moving train. We must catch up, get on track by getting back to basics, then jump on board through obedience and repentance of what the worldly Church has been passing off as righteous practices. Through no fault of our own, this is the state of affairs and has been for centuries. As such, if we want the prize it is of course on us to search out what was lost and not just go along with what is out there.

In reality, in going along with the contemporary church we have jumped on board the Titanic. It is a sinking ship in an ocean of people who are drowning. We were once one of those people that comprise the ocean, and thought ourselves safe once we climbed on board. However the integrity of this ship, the contemporary church, has been compromised and corrupted. As massive, beautiful, and luxurious as it is, it leads us to believe it has got to be right, not flawed. The reality is, however, it too is sinking. Once aboard we must not stand still, but find a lifeboat, even a life vest, which will float, before we go down with the ship and endure the great tribulation.

Our role in our own salvation is more than we bargained for, and will take proactive diligence to find out for ourselves. Our first assignment in becoming followers of Christ is to search out how to follow Christ, while taking it for granted that the Church does not actually know what that looks like. Obviously the reform churches fell short of getting all the way there even if they are separate from the Roman Church. The proof is because the contemporary church is still in the dark and does not know exactly how to understand what the end has in store for us Christians. They do not understand Revelation and cannot agree with what it means. They are slotted for Jesus coming to them like a thief, unaware!

Sadly, things have been this way since Constantine helped set up and organize Church leadership modeling it after the government of the beast, like the Roman senate. That is a structure which by its very nature causes us to eventually follow men more than God. That is opposed to following the Holy Spirit within, while acting in agreement with men what the Spirit is saying.

The Church has let Jesus down, causing Jesus to count on each individual to find the truth as it witnesses to them personally. Coincidently, this is the true nature of the New Covenant relationship in the first place. The New Covenant relationship is relating to God through each individual's conscience.

Amp Jer 31:33 *But this is the covenant which I will make with the house of Israel: After those days, says the Lord,* <u>*I will put My law within them, and on their hearts will I write it; and I will be*</u> <u>*their God, and they will be My people.*</u>
Amp Jer 31:34 *And they will no more teach each man his neighbor and each man his brother,* <u>*saying, Know the Lord, for they will all know Me [recognize, understand, and be acquainted*</u> <u>*with Me], from the least of them to the greatest, says the Lord.*</u> *For I will forgive their iniquity, and I will [seriously] remember their sin no more.*

Amp Ro 7:6 *But now we are discharged from the Law and have terminated all intercourse with it, having died to what once restrained and held us captive.* <u>*So now we serve not under*</u> <u>*[obedience to] the old code of written regulations, but [under obedience to the promptings] of*</u> <u>*the Spirit in newness [of life].*</u>

NIV 1Co 10:29 *. . . For why should my freedom be judged by another's conscience?*

NIV Ro 14:4 <u>*Who are you to judge someone else's servant?*</u> *To his own master he stands or falls. And he will stand, for the Lord is able to make him stand.*

NIV Ro 14:10 <u>*You, then, why do you judge your brother?*</u> *Or why do you look down on your brother? For we will all stand before God's judgment seat.*

NIV Ro 14:11 *It is written: " 'As surely as I live,' says the Lord, 'every knee will bow before me; every tongue will confess to God.' "*

NIV Ro 14:12 *So then, each of us will give an account of himself to God.*

NIV Ro 14:13 <u>*Therefore let us stop passing judgment on one another.*</u> *Instead, make up your mind not to put any stumbling block or obstacle in your brother's way.*

There was one group of church reformers who did finally find what was lost. They were the Quakers, the Church of Philadelphia. They finally remembered, repented and obeyed as admonished by Jesus in the seven letters. The ones not far behind them were the Puritans and the Pilgrims. However, including the Puritans and the Pilgrims, the balance of the Church reformers could not climb up on top of the shoulders of the Quakers in order to continue searching out, or "remembering" that which was from the beginning.

Because the Puritans, and the Pilgrims took a stand against the Quakers, they themselves derailed, becoming stagnant, unable to fully recover what had been lost. Even the Quakers over time have fragmented, and it is the smallest group of the Quakers after fragmenting who still "hang on to their crown of glory," retaining that which they returned to. Jesus was right when He stated that they are "few" "who have not soiled their clothes" in these ages.

The next question is: How can I find what was lost when I personally never knew what it was in the first place? The Lord has provided by throwing out the life preservers in order to pull us back in! Starting in the fifth Church age the Lord released His voices and prophets, calling us out, telling us what was wrong with the Church at large. At the sacrifice of many lives the Lord got the sacred Scriptures back into the hands of the people. Most importantly, it is in our own hearts through our conscience that the Spirit we are born again with teaches and guides us in every area of life. However, we must have a clean heart in that we must desire to know, and we must want Jesus as our first love. That is so we are inspired and motivated to, above all things, search the truth out refining it until our last breath. We cannot do it half heartedly, but we must with all of our heart, mind, soul and strength seek out the Lord.

Amp Da 12:3 *And the teachers and those who are wise shall shine like the brightness of the firmament, and* those who turn many to righteousness (to uprightness and right standing with God) [shall give forth light] like the stars forever and ever.

Amp Da 12:4 *But you, O Daniel, shut up the words and seal the Book until the time of the end.* [Then] many shall run to and fro and search anxiously [through the Book] (search back and forth through the Scriptures), and knowledge [of God's purposes as revealed by His prophets] shall be increased and become great.

The Vision which Follows the Seven Letters

As with all of God's words we can count on Revelation being the undiluted truth of exactly how it was, how it is, and how it will be. Everything that Jesus speaks in a direct manner to the churches in the seven letters we are shown the reality of His words through the prophetic visions that follow. However, in comparison to the seven letters, the scope of these visions reach back further in time to the beginning and go beyond to the end of time.

The seven letters are focused exclusively on the history of the Church Age in the earth. The time of the Church Age is revealed to us in the 70-7's told to us in Daniel. The Church Age is the gap between the 69th-7 and the final 1-7. It is a gap which is necessitated by the rejection of the Jews of their place as the "bride" (the celestial humans who are to reign with Christ for 1,000 years from the New Jerusalem). The Church Age began when the 62-7's ended. That would be in 33 AD when the Jews had Jesus killed. When the Church Age ends, the last 7 will resume. Then, 7 years later will conclude the 70-7's.

Revelation begins with Jesus' letters to the Church concerning the entire Church Age. Reading the 7 letters in context to the entire scope of the Church Age brings a seriousness to the admonishment and disappointments Jesus expresses about His bride. In them, He repeatedly warns her to wake up before it is too late. These letters which precede the visions are written in a completely different style of writing. They are in a direct dialogue form, personal, and intimate. These letters are, however, by the very nature of how the Lord sees; prophetically. Jesus frames what He says in a holistic way from outside of time, from its essence to its conclusion. Volume 2 gave the meaning of the seven letters according to a prophetically historical context showing us a whole new layer of what the Lord was communicating to us—His bride and Church.

In Volumes 3 through 6 we will go through the visions and their 4 respective narratives line by line. One volume will be devoted to each of the four narratives, starting with this Volume 3.

Here are a few tips to keep in mind when trying to understand the visions of Revelation: It is important to recognize that the Bible starts with the sevenness of creation and ends with the sevenness of that creation's conclusion. It is wise to look at the number seven like it is used for the number of days in a week and how it is used in creation in order to understand how it is used in Revelation. On the one hand, it is obviously used in a quantitive way because there are actually seven days in a week. After the seven days of creation, the creation was complete. On the other hand, God said that it was good (perfection). Which describes the sevenness of creation or the meaning given the number seven by God.

These series of visions tell a story. However, it is a mistake to think that just because they are visions they tell us only of what is to come in the future. Although they are prophecy regarding the future they are also prophetic insight into history as well. That's why we say it tells a story. Knowing this, we can resist the temptation of trying to make all the elements of the visions relate only to something to come in the future. In turn, it will help in not skewing the proper meanings of the elements and aid in giving proper points of references over the timeline they speak within.

We have already covered the *structure of sevens* in Volume 1, *Introduction to Revelation* when it was explained that to use the number 7 means the entire scope of the subject matter is being revealed (from its very essence to its end). The entire scope of what a vision encapsulates aids a great deal in being able to form a context of the messages within the visions. Conversely, to skew the scope of a vision believing, for example, that all of it pertains to something in the future, will make it impossible to form a context and interpret the vision.

Revelation is a series of visions within a heavenly encounter. In the course of recording these visions John often starts with, "after this I looked," "after this I saw," "then I saw," or "then I heard." In order to follow the true outline of this series of visions John is having, it is important to understand that "after this", or "then I saw" doesn't mean the next thing in chronological order as a part of the last thing I saw. It's like him saying in other words that, "After this intense vision, I saw this vision." It's more like saying, "The previous one just finished and now I was being shown this other one."

To say things like; "after" or "then I saw," actually signifies a transition that one vision had finished and now I was being shown the next one. It is like John is being barraged with one vision after another from every direction. He no more finishes seeing one vision, of which undoes his person having endured the emotional and spiritual intensity and trauma of it, then from over the other shoulder to see another equally intense vision. Then another, and another from different directions barely having time to take in all it incites within his heart before seeing the next. Is it any wonder that after the experience is over John collapses at the feet of one of the angels showing him all this?

WEB Rev 22:8 ... *When I heard and saw* (these visions), *I fell down to worship before the feet of the angel who had shown me these things.*

John had to be completely undone with no strength left in his person, totally overloaded intellectually, emotionally, and spiritually. What he saw was in the fullness of the whole world in all its time, past, present, and future. It was also the fullness of its hate, murder, desperation, torment, delusion, pain, suffering, lust, power, betrayal, evil, love, sacrifice, judgment, and mercy for all time for the whole earth. This is something of a burden no one man which has only one life time could possibly bear in a single dose. Only with supernatural strength could it have been possible to take in the sheer emotional and spiritual weight of this knowledge.

With few exceptions, all prophecy has a regional and contemporary manifestation as well as a global and end times manifestation. Understanding this will avoid getting confused in thinking that this prophecy has already been fulfilled. In fact, when there is a regional and contemporary manifestation of prophecy, it becomes an affirmation that such a thing will occur on a global scale during the end times. So, it does no good to start saying for example, in the case of Antiochus, there was already the abomination that caused desolation in the temple during the 2nd century BC. Knowing the case of Antiochus, Jesus still told us what Daniel predicted in Da 9:27, and what Antiochus fulfilled in Da 8:9-14, will happen again at the end on a global scale.

Before beginning, here is something important to point out. In Volumes 3 through 6 the whole book of Revelation is read beginning with chapter four. However, for the sake of interpretation many supporting or repeated Scriptures are also used as an aid. To make it easier to follow, the continuous reading of the book of Revelation is highlighted with grey. Scriptures which are repeated or are out of their place, or any other Bible Scriptures used are not highlighted. That is so there may be a distinction between the Scriptures used for explanations and interpretation purposes, from those used for the actual reading of Revelation from chapter four to the end. Also, if articles are quoted, the text of the articles will be indented with a smaller font size.

Read only the Scriptures highlighted with grey then you have a continuous and uninterrupted copy of the book of Revelation from chapter 4:1 to the end of the book.

It is a unique and confusing way Revelation is laid out. It is the story of the world from its beginning to its end. It covers its corruption, its fall, its redemption, and punishment. However, once you discover where the four different narratives begin and end, in addition to grasping the overall context, timelines, subjects and outline, they begin to make perfect sense. Then, given you understand the symbolic meaning of the elements, it begins to read like a blueprint. In the next chapter we will begin the first of the four narratives, *The Seven Seals*.

CHAPTER 2

The Throne in Heaven

Let's begin with the narrative and timeline of the story of the world as told by the Lord and recorded by John.

The Throne in Heaven

> WEB Rev 4:1 *After these things I looked and saw a door opened in heaven, and the first voice that I heard, like a trumpet speaking with me, was one saying, "Come up here, and I will show you the things which must happen after this." 2 Immediately I was in the Spirit. Behold, there was a throne set in heaven, and one sitting on the throne 3 that looked like a jasper stone and a sardius. There was a rainbow around the throne, like an emerald to look at.*

Let's compare Rev 4:1-2 (above) with the description John gives of when he first encounters Jesus in Rev 1:10-18 (below) when John was asked to take down the letters to the seven churches:

WEB Rev 1:10 *I was in the Spirit on the Lord's day, and I heard behind me a loud voice, like a trumpet 11 saying, "(I am the Alpha and the Omega, the First and the Last) What you see, write in a book (scroll) and send to the seven assemblies (churches): to Ephesus, Smyrna, Pergamum, Thyatira, Sardis, Philadelphia, and to Laodicea." 12 I turned to see the voice that spoke with me. Having turned, I saw seven golden lamp stands. 13 And among the lamp stands was one like a son of man, clothed with a robe reaching down to his feet, and with a golden sash around his chest. 14 His head and his hair were white as white wool, like snow. His eyes were like a flame of fire. 15 His feet were like burnished brass (bronze), as if it had been refined in a furnace. His voice was like the voice of many waters.* [16] *He had seven stars in his right hand. Out of his mouth proceeded a sharp two-edged sword. His face was like the sun shining at its brightest.* [17] *When I saw him, I fell at his feet like a dead man. He laid his right hand on me, saying, "Don't be afraid. I am the first and the last,* [18] *and the Living one. I was dead, and behold, I am alive forever more. Amen. I have the keys of Death and of Hades.*

This was an encounter with heaven and not just a mere vision. At the beginning of this encounter it started with John quiet, still, in prayer, and in a lucid spiritual state. Suddenly, interrupting the silence from behind, he hears a voice which is so loud it is like the blast of a trumpet, and so full it is like the sound of rushing waters—like a water fall. When John turns around to see where this sound comes from he sees a scene which is the sight of Jesus in heaven before the throne where the seven lampstands have their place. Again, this is not a vision but an encounter with heaven. It is there behind him very close. We know because he is so startled he falls at the feet of Jesus as if dead. In addition, Jesus reaches down to him and places His hand on John to calm and strengthen him. Imagine, whatever was behind John as he prayed, a wall or furniture perhaps, even the ceiling of a small room, however, it is no longer there, but instead heaven right there within the reach of his hands before the feet of Jesus.

After taking down what Jesus wanted written in the letters to the seven churches there is a huge transition. Behind him the scene he saw was not there anymore. Instead there above is a door open to heaven, open to a different dimension, the spiritual realm which is also outside of time and space. It is the same voice of whose feet he was just before who is now calling him from beyond that door to come up.

WEB Rev 4:1 After these things I looked and saw a door opened in heaven, and the first voice that I heard, like a trumpet speaking with me, was one saying, "Come up here, and I will show you the things which must happen after this." ² Immediately I was in the Spirit. Behold, there was a throne set in heaven, and one sitting on the throne . . .

John starts the encounter with a tear in the fabric of space and time with everything taken away that stands between the throne of God and him on earth in a prison work camp. With it so close he can touch the feet of Jesus and Jesus can touch him. Then, it is gone. The only trace of it being the voice he heard calling to him from behind a door, which suddenly transports him to heaven in the spiritual dimension before the throne room. This is the opposite of how this started. Heaven came to him and spoke to John telling him of the things he was supposed to express to the Church. Now, he must go to heaven, the spiritual realm outside of space and time from where he was beckoned, because the same voice told him to show (not tell) him the things which must happen. To show John, Jesus had to take him outside of space and most importantly time, so that from beginning to end he could see with his own eyes.

This is fantastic! Can this really happen? Can the fabric of space and time be torn and everything between the throne of God in the spirit realm and a man on the earth in the natural realm be removed? Here is an eyewitness account which says a resounding yes! This fact becomes very important when it comes to what happens when the sixth seal is broken.

WEB Rev 4:3 ... *There was a rainbow around the throne, like an emerald to look at.*

The rainbow was set there like an "emerald to look at," or like a ring displayed on one's finger to adorn oneself with. To gaze upon God on His throne, is to gaze upon the beauty of that rainbow which encircles God, and the authority of His throne. It is there for all to see. It is a boundary that God self-imposed upon Himself limiting His authority/power and displaying that boundary keeping Him accountable to it for all to see. To see God is synonymous with knowing His promises.

According to the *structure of sevens* in Revelation, within each vision we should be able to see the beginning and end of the subject of the vision. That is because seven means completion, meaning everything about the subject is contained within the sevenness of it. The rainbow is a sign reminding God of His promise not to destroy the inhabitants of the earth again with a great flood. The rainbow being here is a significant element to the vision. It gives us a starting point with which to have context concerning the seven seals. That starting point is after His promise after the flood, and the start of the "new beginning"—the repopulation of the earth on dry land by the eight who came out of the ark.

WEB Rev 4:1 ... *I will show you the things which must happen after this.*

"After this" means after what John now sees in that place beyond time after he was immediately taken up in the spirit and was before the throne. What he sees is the Father on His throne with a rainbow encircling it. I will show you what must take place after the promise I made and am bound with by the rainbow. This is a different type of use than how "after this I saw" is used, as we talked about in the introduction. This scene John sees is no ordinary work day in the court of heaven. John has not only transcended from the natural realm to the spiritual realm before the throne while still alive in the body, but also transcends time in order to be shown an event which took/takes place in heaven. An event which allows him to see past, present, and future events on earth.

What is this event? It is an event which takes place in court when a decision or verdict has been handed down from the Father. Outside of time John is able to witness the execution of it. A decision which can only be both revealed and executed by His Christ, because it is one of both judgment and redemption. What was this verdict? It was judgment against the world for the second time. The first being the flood when the LORD lamented:

NIV Ge 6:5 The LORD saw how great man's wickedness on the earth had become, and that every inclination of the thoughts of his heart was only evil all the time.
NIV Ge 6:6 The LORD was grieved that he had made man on the earth, and his heart was filled with pain.
NIV Ge 6:7 So the LORD said, "I will wipe mankind, whom I have created, from the face of the earth—men and animals, and creatures that move along the ground, and birds of the air—for I am grieved that I have made them."

At that time only eight people survived that judgment and no one was redeemed. That occasion was more like a second chance for humanity to start over again.

On this second occasion of administered judgment we will find the judgment will turn out thorough, absolute, and final. However, there is a redemption of man involved. This judgment is so complete that all which was created in the first seven days of Genesis comes to a complete and utter destruction in a fire. The universe is not allowed to live out its time—its natural course of life, but is like a condemned criminal sentenced with capital punishment with its natural life cut short.

Amp 2Pe 3:10 *But the day of the Lord will come like a thief* (the last day when resurrection of the dead will occur and all will be judged), *and then the heavens will vanish (pass away) with a thunderous crash, and the [material] elements [of the universe] will be dissolved with fire, and the earth and the works that are upon it will be burned up.*

Amp 2Pe 3:11 *Since* <u>*all these things are thus in the process of being dissolved,*</u> *what kind of person ought [each of] you to be [in the meanwhile] in consecrated and holy behavior and devout and godly qualities,*

Amp 2Pe 3:12 *While you wait and earnestly long for (expect and hasten) the coming of the day of God by reason of which the flaming heavens will be dissolved, and the [material] elements [of the universe] will flare and melt with fire?*

Amp 2Pe 3:13 <u>*But we look for new heavens and a new earth according to His promise, in which*</u> <u>*righteousness (uprightness, freedom from sin, and right standing with God) is to abide.*</u>

> *WEB Rev 4:4* *Around the throne were twenty-four thrones. On the thrones were twenty-four elders sitting, dressed in white garments, with crowns of gold on their heads. 5 Out of the throne proceed lightnings, sounds, and thunders. There were seven lamps of fire burning before his throne, which are the seven Spirits of God.*

The twenty-four elders are the heavenly witnesses in the court of God. They are the court witnesses to all which the LORD decides and carries out (among whatever other responsibilities they may have).

"There were seven lamps of fire burning . . ." Although this is an occasion of judgment, God does so while making a way of redemption. From the seven letters we already know that the lampstands have within them the Spirit of the bride, which will cause believers to become celestial beings in union with Christ. This actually tells us that God is not just out to destroy, but to redeem all who would be redeemed.

NLT Eze 18:23 *"Do you think, asks the Sovereign LORD, that I like to see wicked people die? Of course not! I only want them to turn from their wicked ways and live.*

NLT 2Pe 3:9 *The Lord isn't really being slow about his promise to return, as some people think. No, he is being patient for your sake. He does not want anyone to perish, so he is giving more time for everyone to repent.*

With the above being the case God uses His judgment not just to bring all corruption to an end, but to unfold it in a way that through His judgment He uses the corrupt to distinguish and purify the redeemed—the wheat from the darnel. God exploits the enmity between the line of offspring of the Devil and the line of offspring of Eve. This verdict and judgment has been painstakingly engineered to produce and redeem man—the ones He made in His own image. These seven lamps are the seven Spirits and seven ages of the Church Age, as well as representing the churches themselves or those within the Church who will eventually possess the fullness of the seven Spirits in those lampstands.

WEB Rev 4:6a *Before the throne was something like a sea of glass, similar to crystal.*

The "sea of glass" is another example of an element mentioned in this vision which only later can we get a full appreciation of its interpretive meaning. "Before the throne was something like a sea of glass." This sea of glass is like a boundary or portal into the sea of humanity in the natural world. It is when this same sea of glass comes up again that we can know what it is.

NIV Rev 15:1 *I saw in heaven another great and marvelous sign: seven angels with the seven last plagues—last, because with them God's wrath is completed.*
NIV Rev 15:2 *And I saw what looked like a sea of glass mixed with fire and, standing beside the sea, those who had been victorious over the beast and his image and over the number of his name. They held harps given them by God*
NIV Rev 15:3 *and sang the song of Moses the servant of God and the song of the Lamb:*

We see on this occasion the elect who died for the name of Jesus during the great tribulation are watching what takes place on the earth from heaven in the spiritual dimension through the portal called, "the sea of glass." They are watching humanity burn in the retribution of God's wrath for having killed the elect who watch this happen singing and celebrating the event.

What a vision! John sees the throne of the Lord, with the heavenly elders seated around Him on their thrones. And the magnificent living creatures in their place. His promise to Noah bound around Him and His throne in the form of a beautiful rainbow. The promise of His bride already created and ablaze with life in the form of the seven lampstands. Before Him and His throne is a portal by which the activities of humanity in the natural realm can be seen. It is a crystal like transparent glass curtain which allows Him to see all that occurs in the world past, present, and future—all from outside of time in heaven.

> *WEB Rev 4:6b In the middle of the throne, and around the throne were four living creatures full of eyes before and behind. ⁷ The first creature was like a lion, and the second creature like a calf, and the third creature had a face like a man, and the fourth was like a flying eagle. ⁸ The four living creatures, each one of them having six wings, are full of eyes around and within. They have no rest day and night, saying, "Holy, holy, holy is the Lord God, the Almighty, who was and who is and who is to come!"*
>
> *⁹ When the living creatures give glory, honor, and thanks to him who sits on the throne, to him who lives forever and ever, ¹⁰ the twenty-four elders fall down before him who sits on the throne, and worship him who lives forever and ever, and throw their crowns before the throne, saying, ¹¹ "Worthy are you, our Lord and God, the Holy One, to receive the glory, the honor, and the power, for you created all things, and because of your desire they existed, and were created!"*

Here is an interesting factor to take note of those who surround the throne of the Lord. This spectacle of awe starts with the twenty-four elders and the four living creatures and the seven lampstands which is the Spirit of His bride, the church future. We will see that as this scene is revisited or as time progresses through the events of the seven seals, the numbers surrounding the throne will increase. The reason for the increase is always because of the activities and redeeming works of the Lord which precede new numbers before Him praising and thanking Him for all that He has done. It is a "great multitude" who will populate heaven and survive the destruction of the universe becoming celestial humans whose habitat was formerly in the natural universe.

CHAPTER 3

The Scroll and the Lamb

WEB Rev 5:1 I saw, in the right hand of him who sat on the throne, a book (scroll) written inside and outside, sealed shut with seven seals. ² I saw a mighty angel proclaiming with a loud voice, "Who is worthy to open the book (scroll), and to break its seals?"

W ho is it that is sitting on the throne holding the scroll in His right hand? It is God in heaven, the Father of the only begotten Son! The heavenly Sanhedrin is seated in their place of authority and all are giving praise to the Father (4:8-11) who is on the throne with a scroll in His right hand. Jesus has been last sighted as walking among the lampstands. With hair like wool white as snow and eyes like flames of fire, wearing a white robe down to His feet with a golden sash draped over Him, and feet which look like burnished bronze in a furnace.

Who is the one standing in the center of the throne? It is the Son who is fully God and had become also the Son of Man with God as His Father. Fully God and fully man.

WEB Rev 5:3 No one in heaven above, or on the earth, or under the earth, was able to open the book (scroll), or to look in it. ⁴ And I wept much, because no one was found worthy to open the book (scroll), or to look in it. ⁵ One of the elders said to me, "Don't weep. Behold, the Lion who is of the tribe of Judah, the Root of David, has overcome; he who opens the book (scroll) and its seven seals." ⁶ I saw in the middle of the throne (in the center of the court before the throne) and of the four living creatures, and in the middle of the elders, a Lamb standing, as though it had been slain (literally: I saw a Lamb with its throat cut), having seven horns, and seven eyes, which are the seven Spirits of God, sent out into all the earth.

The book of Revelation started out with these words:

NIV Rev 1:1 The revelation of Jesus Christ, which God gave him to show his servants what must soon take place. He made it known by sending his angel to his servant John,
NIV Rev 1:2 who testifies to everything he saw—that is, the word of God and the testimony of Jesus Christ.
NIV Rev 1:3 Blessed is the one who reads the words of this prophecy, and blessed are those who hear it and take to heart what is written in it, because the time is near.

When it says this is "the revelation of Jesus Christ which God gave Him," it means the entire vision of Revelation which Jesus passed on to John is what God the Father gave to Jesus. Revelation means; that which has been revealed or disclosed, with an implication that it will enlighten the recipient with its information. The Father gave to Jesus a vision of the things to come. He did so that Jesus could make His people know everything which would take place in the future so that His bride, His Church would not be in the dark concerning what the future holds or how to embrace it and survive it. Neither would they be in the dark concerning why what was going to happen, had to happen. The unfolding of time and the fate of the world is and will be something that simply befalls humankind. They will not understand the "what" or "why," but be forced to accept, adapt, and finally succumb to everything that befalls them.

The Father enlightened His son Jesus, the only One worthy of knowing and the One worthy of knowing first before anyone else. We see highlighted in the vision how this is true when John weeps because no one is found worthy of knowing the contents. It is only Him who is worthy, Him who would give His life as a sacrifice for others to have eternal life, the Father's own Son! Jesus gave to John through the angel the vision His Father gave to Him. In turn, John, the Lord's servant, was to make it known to the Church. Because of this, the vision of Revelation is the testimony of Jesus, and His testimony (the vision of Revelation) is the spirit of prophecy. When John fell at the feet of the angel that Jesus sent to give this vision to him, this is what he said:

NIV Rev 19:9 Then the angel said to me, "Write: 'Blessed are those who are invited to the wedding supper of the Lamb!' " And he added, "These are the true words of God."

NIV Rev 19:10 *At this I fell at his feet to worship him. But he said to me, "Do not do it!I am a* *fellow servant with you and with your brothers who hold to the testimony of Jesus. Worship* *God! For the testimony of Jesus is the spirit of prophecy."*

The angel also said:

NIV Rev 22:6 *The angel said to me, "These words are trustworthy and true. The Lord, the God of* *the spirits of the prophets, sent his angel to show his servants the things that must soon take* *place."*

Revelation is the testimony of Jesus, and the testimony of Jesus is the spirit of prophecy, making Jesus "the God of the spirits of the prophets" who informs His Church (for example, John). The fact that the Father wanted this communicated to the bride of Christ, coupled with the knowledge that Jesus alone was worthy to receive it and then pass it on, tells us something very important. There are many human voices that tell us of what will happen in the future, however, these verses tell us only one person was worthy to hear the plan of the Father. That person is Jesus. What that tells us is Jesus knows and all of the others are speculating. Whatever they claim to know did not come from the Father of all creation. Even if they claim they received their prophecy from heavenly angelic beings. We know this because it is said right here no one in heaven or on earth was worthy to be privy to God's plan except the One who sacrificed himself for those who the Father wanted to inform— His bride.

Furthermore, it is important to note that the Father would not have Jesus or His bride, the Church, in the dark concerning His plans for the whole earth. The Father's love, affection, and intimacy towards His Son is demonstrated very clearly in this part. Likewise, because it is His Son's bride and they (the Church) are of one Spirit with His Son, the Father extends the same level of intimacy, affection, and love towards her by giving Jesus the vision of Revelation to pass onto her. The Father respects and loves the Church, He gave His Son's life for her to be redeemed.

It must not be ignored that the vision called Revelation starts out with John weeping because its information cannot be disclosed. Why make a point of this when John was called up for the very reason of seeing what must take place? The Father and God of everything wants it to be clear how He embraces His Son, and His bride. He wants them to know their special status, and privilege, because of our Christ.

By highlighting this we should always believe that if we are in union with Christ, fate and the future is never anything that we should not already know before it happens, because of the Father's love for us. However, if we do not know, or if we know and do not understand, this tells us something about our union, our status and privilege.

The state of the Church today is a statement of the status of our union with Jesus given we do not understand the book of Revelation or the fact that the spirit of prophecy has been dead in the Church for the longest time! It unequivocally means our union with Christ is not what we imagine it to be. It is under this condition which Jesus told His Church that:

NIV Rev 3:15 I know your deeds, that you are neither cold nor hot. I wish you were either one or the other!
NIV Rev 3:16 So, because you are lukewarm—neither hot nor cold—I am about to spit you out of my mouth.
NIV Rev 3:17 You say, 'I am rich; I have acquired wealth and do not need a thing.' But you do not realize that you are wretched, pitiful, poor, blind and naked.
NIV Rev 3:18 I counsel you to buy from me gold refined in the fire, so you can become rich; and white clothes to wear, so you can cover your shameful nakedness; and salve to put on your eyes, so you can see.
NIV Rev 3:19 Those whom I love I rebuke and discipline. So be earnest, and repent.

And again:

NIV Rev 3:2 Wake up! Strengthen what remains and is about to die, for I have not found your deeds complete in the sight of my God.
NIV Rev 3:3 Remember, therefore, what you have received and heard; obey it, and repent. But if you do not wake up, I will come like a thief, and you will not know at what time I will come to you.

I once heard a leader of an evangelical church tell me that prophecy was no longer among us and it is the case because God gave us the written word—the Bible. The spirit of prophecy had left the Church when the written word came in its place. That way flawed and imperfect men who might speak for God will not make a mistake because it is now written in black and white, as the evangelical claimed. However, John painstakingly tried to make us understand that the written word of God, jumped off the pages and became flesh (Jn 1:14), a living talking being we could speak to, rendering the written word obsolete.

NIV Heb 8:1 The point of what we are saying is this: We do have such a high priest, who sat down at the right hand of the throne of the Majesty in heaven,

NIV Heb 8:2 and who serves in the sanctuary, the true tabernacle set up by the Lord, not by man.

NIV Heb 8:3 Every high priest is appointed to offer both gifts and sacrifices, and so it was necessary for this one also to have something to offer.

NIV Heb 8:4 If he were on earth, he would not be a priest, for there are already men who offer the gifts prescribed by the law.

NIV Heb 8:5 They serve at a sanctuary that is a copy and shadow of what is in heaven. This is why Moses was warned when he was about to build the tabernacle: "See to it that you make everything according to the pattern shown you on the mountain."

NIV Heb 8:6 But the ministry Jesus has received is as superior to theirs as the covenant of which he is mediator is superior to the old one, and it is founded on better promises.

NIV Heb 8:7 For if there had been nothing wrong with that first covenant, no place would have been sought for another.

NIV Heb 8:8 But God found fault with the people and said: "The time is coming, declares the Lord, when I will make a new covenant with the house of Israel and with the house of Judah.

NIV Heb 8:9 It will not be like the covenant I made with their forefathers when I took them by the hand to lead them out of Egypt, because they did not remain faithful to my covenant, and I turned away from them, declares the Lord.

NIV Heb 8:10 This is the covenant I will make with the house of Israel after that time, declares the Lord. I will put my laws in their minds and write them on their hearts. I will be their God, and they will be my people.

NIV Heb 8:11 No longer will a man teach his neighbor, or a man his brother, saying, 'Know the Lord,' because they will all know me, from the least of them to the greatest.

NIV Heb 8:12 *For I will forgive their wickedness and will remember their sins no more."*
NIV Heb 8:13 *By calling this covenant "new," he has made the first one obsolete; and what is obsolete and aging will soon disappear.*

Likewise, the Apostles taught us that no longer was the presence of God's Spirit in one stone building, but in many buildings of flesh. We, who are in union with Him, are the temple and voice of God. If you have seen us, you have seen God, because we posses His Spirit and have died to our own life in the body giving His Spirit expression through our own life and body.

NIV 1Co 6:19 *Do you not know that your body is a temple of the Holy Spirit, who is in you, whom you have received from God? You are not your own;*
NIV 1Co 6:20 *you were bought at a price. Therefore honor God with your body.*

NIV 1Pe 4:6 *For this is the reason the gospel was preached even to those who are now dead, so that they might be judged according to men in regard to the body, but live according to God in regard to the spirit.*
NIV 1Pe 4:7 *The end of all things is near. Therefore be clear minded and self-controlled so that you can pray.*
NIV 1Pe 4:8 *Above all, love each other deeply, because love covers over a multitude of sins.*
NIV 1Pe 4:9 *Offer hospitality to one another without grumbling.*
NIV 1Pe 4:10 *Each one should use whatever gift he has received to serve others, faithfully administering God's grace in its various forms.*
NIV 1Pe 4:11 *If anyone speaks, he should do it as one speaking the very words of God. If anyone serves, he should do it with the strength God provides, so that in all things God may be praised through Jesus Christ. To him be the glory and the power for ever and ever. Amen.*

Amp Ro 7:6 *But now we are discharged from the Law and have terminated all intercourse with it, having died to what once restrained and held us captive. So now we serve not under [obedience to] the old code of written regulations, but [under obedience to the promptings] of the Spirit in newness [of life].*

The real answer of why prophecy is dead for the bigger part of the Church is not the convenient reason that evangelical church leader gave. Jesus tells us why. He is divorcing the Church, spewing them out of His mouth (Rev 3:16), removing their lampstand (Rev 2:5) and coming against them with the sword of His mouth (Rev

2:16), and in doing so He will come as a thief and the *Church Corrupt* who lost their first love will not be aware (Rev 3:3), or know as the *Church Pure* who is in union with Him.

The seven horns of the Lamb are the seven Church ages and the power granted the Lamb over them. Or you could say those seven horns are the sevenness of His power over the Church, His bride, during the Church Age. It is just as with the seven heads of the beast with his ten horns and seven crowns; or the crown of twelve stars on the head of the woman clothed with the sun, Eve.

The seven eyes of the Lamb represent the Holy Spirit, or the Spirit of the bride, even Jesus' own Spirit. The seven eyes represent the seven ages or "sevenness" of the Church Age. Jesus' eyes are like a blazing fire which illuminate everything He looks upon. Our eyes see light reflected off an object. If there is no light to illuminate it, we cannot see it, it remains in the darkness to us. When Jesus looks at an object His sight lightens it, illuminating every aspect of it.

NLT Heb 4:12 For the word of God is full of living power. It is sharper than the sharpest knife, cutting deep into our innermost thoughts and desires. It exposes us for what we really are. NLT Heb 4:13 Nothing in all creation can hide from him. Everything is naked and exposed before his eyes. This is the God to whom we must explain all that we have done.

That is because His Spirit is light, it is the light and consciousness of men.

NIV Jn 1:4 In him was life, and that life was the light of men. NIV Jn 1:5 The light shines in the darkness, but the darkness has not understood it.

The seven eyes of the Lamb is the fullness or the sevenness of the/His Holy Spirit in the earth in the hearts of the believers who possess His Spirit. Likewise, who through His illuminating light/vision sees and exposes the heart motives of those still in the darkness upon the earth. Jesus does not need the sea of glass before the throne, His Spirit in His Church illuminates and convicts the hearts of those still in the darkness through the eyes of their hearts.

Amp Eph 1:17 [For I always pray to] the God of our Lord Jesus Christ, the Father of glory, that He may grant you a spirit of wisdom and revelation [of insight into mysteries and secrets] in the [deep and intimate] knowledge of Him,

Amp Eph 1:18 By having the eyes of your heart flooded with light, so that you can know and understand the hope to which He has called you, and how rich is His glorious inheritance in the saints (His set-apart ones),

Amp Eph 1:19 And [so that you can know and understand] what is the immeasurable and unlimited and surpassing greatness of His power in and for us who believe, as demonstrated in the working of His mighty strength,

Amp Eph 1:20 Which He exerted in Christ when He raised Him from the dead and seated Him at His [own] right hand in the heavenly [places],

Amp Eph 1:21 Far above all rule and authority and power and dominion and every name that is named [above every title that can be conferred], not only in this age and in this world, but also in the age and the world which are to come.

Amp Eph 1:22 And He has put all things under His feet and has appointed Him the universal and supreme Head of the church [a headship exercised throughout the church],

Amp Eph 1:23 Which is His body, the fullness (or sevenness) of Him Who fills all in all [for in that body lives the full measure of Him Who makes everything complete, and Who fills everything everywhere with Himself].

Amp Eph 2:1 AND YOU [He made alive], when you were dead (slain) by [your] trespasses and sins.

This is all very important to grasp. The verses below explain how the illuminating light shines through the eyes of those in union with Jesus, exposing and convicting the hidden things of those who are still in darkness.

Amp Jn 3:16 For God so greatly loved and dearly prized the world that He [even] gave up His only begotten (unique) Son, so that whoever believes in (trusts in, clings to, relies on) Him shall not perish (come to destruction, be lost) but have eternal (everlasting) life.

Amp Jn 3:17 For God did not send the Son into the world in order to judge (to reject, to condemn, to pass sentence on) the world, but that the world might find salvation and be made safe and sound through Him.

Amp Jn 3:18 He who believes in Him [who clings to, trusts in, relies on Him] is not judged [he who trusts in Him never comes up for judgment; for him there is no rejection, no condemnation—he incurs no damnation]; but he who does not believe (cleave to, rely on, trust in Him) is judged already [he has already been convicted and has already received his *sentence] because he has not believed in and trusted in the name of the only begotten Son of God. [He is condemned for refusing to let his trust rest in Christ's name.]*

Amp Jn 3:19 The [basis of the] judgment (indictment, the test by which men are judged, the ground for the sentence) lies in this: the Light has come into the world, and people have loved the darkness rather than and more than the Light, for their works (deeds) were evil.

Amp Jn 3:20 For every wrongdoer hates (loathes, detests) the Light, and will not come out into the Light but shrinks from it, lest his works (his deeds, his activities, his conduct) be exposed and reproved.

Amp Jn 3:21 But he who practices truth [who does what is right] comes out into the Light; so that his works may be plainly shown to be what they are—wrought with God [divinely prompted, done with God's help, in dependence upon Him].

And again:

Amp 2Co 3:16 But whenever a person turns [in repentance] to the Lord, the veil is stripped off and taken away.

Amp 2Co 3:17 Now the Lord is the Spirit, and where the Spirit of the Lord is, there is liberty (emancipation from bondage, freedom).

Amp 2Co 3:18 And all of us, as with unveiled face, [because we] continued to behold [in the Word of God] as in a mirror the glory of the Lord, are constantly being transfigured into His very own image in ever increasing splendor and from one degree of glory to another; [for this comes] from the Lord [Who is] the Spirit.

John is told to look at the Lion of the tribe of Judah, the Root of David.

However, when he looks, what he sees is a Lamb with its throat cut. Being outside of time, John watches this vision of several images of Jesus, which have happened throughout time. At this part of the vision, John is shown the risen Jesus who has triumphed through His sacrificial death, showing what He has done to be worthy of opening the scroll with its seven seals.

We are presented with three images of Jesus in this one vision:

1) *WEB Rev 1:13 And among the lamp stands was one like a son of man, clothed with a robe reaching down to his feet, and with a golden sash around his chest. 14 His head and his hair* *were white as white wool, like snow. His eyes were like a flame of fire.* ¹⁵ *His feet were like burnished brass, as if it had been refined in a furnace. His voice was like the voice of many waters.* ¹⁶ *He had seven stars in his right hand. Out of his mouth proceeded a sharp two-edged sword. His face was like the sun shining at its brightest.*

Here John sees Jesus not only as a brother human being, but also as the first born resurrected of the dead, the Lord of lords and King of kings. In addition, Jesus is the head and the Spirit source of His church, the souls who were born again of a new Spirit (recreated as celestial beings).

2) ᵂᴱᴮ ᴿᵉᵛ ⁵:⁵ ... *Behold, the Lion who is of the tribe of Judah, the Root of David ...*

These are two Old Testament titles, the Lion of the tribe of Judah and the Root of David

A) The Lion of the tribe of Judah:

As Jacob/Israel blesses his twelve sons he speaks of their future. The following is what he spoke to his son, Judah:

ᵂᴱᴮ ᴳᵉ ⁴⁹:¹ *Jacob called to his sons, and said: "Gather yourselves together, that I may tell you that which will happen to you in the days to come.*
ᵂᴱᴮ ᴳᵉ ⁴⁹:² *Assemble yourselves, and hear, you sons of Jacob.*
Listen to Israel, your father.

ᵂᴱᴮ ᴳᵉ ⁴⁹:⁸ *"Judah, your brothers will praise you.*
Your hand will be on the neck of your enemies.
Your father's sons will bow down before you.
ᵂᴱᴮ ᴳᵉ ⁴⁹:⁹ *Judah is a lion's cub.*
From the prey, my son, you have gone up.
He stooped down, he crouched as a lion,
as a lioness.
Who will rouse him up?
ᵂᴱᴮ ᴳᵉ ⁴⁹:¹⁰ *The scepter will not depart from Judah,*
nor the ruler's staff from between his feet,
until he comes to whom it belongs.

To him will the obedience of the peoples be (the nations) .
WEB Ge 49:11 *Binding his foal to the vine,*
his donkey's colt to the choice vine;
he has washed his garments in wine,
his robes in the blood of grapes.
WEB Ge 49:12 *His eyes will be red with wine,*
his teeth white with milk.

Above, Jesus is spoken of as the kinsman redeemer of all of Israel. He is the warrior king to which the scepter will never depart from. All the nations will bow down to Him. And He will carry out justice.

B) The Root of David (son of Jesse):

WEB Isa 11:1 *A shoot will come out of the stock of Jesse,*
and a branch out of his roots will bear fruit.
WEB Isa 11:2 *Yahweh's Spirit will rest on him:*
the spirit of wisdom and understanding,
the spirit of counsel and might,
the spirit of knowledge and of the fear of Yahweh.
WEB Isa 11:3a *His delight will be in the fear of Yahweh.*

Fear: Fear is worship. To fear is to yield your will to the will of another's. Jesus delighted in the fear of the LORD meaning; He delighted in surrendering His own will to instead live for and to yield the members of His body to the will of His Father. "If you have seen me you have seen the Father."

WEB Isa 11:3b *He will not judge by the sight of his eyes,*
neither decide by the hearing of his ears;
WEB Isa 11:4 *but with righteousness he will judge the poor,*
and decide with equity for the humble of the earth.
He will strike the earth with the rod of his mouth;
and with the breath of his lips he will kill the wicked.
WEB Isa 11:5 *Righteousness will be the belt of his waist,*
and faithfulness the belt of his waist.

WEB Isa 11:6 *The wolf will live with the lamb,*

and the leopard will lie down with the young goat;

The calf, the young lion, and the fattened calf together;

and a little child will lead them.

WEB Isa 11:7 *The cow and the bear will graze.*

Their young ones will lie down together.

The lion will eat straw like the ox.

WEB Isa 11:8 *The nursing child will play near a cobra's hole,*

and the weaned child will put his hand on the viper's den.

WEB Isa 11:9 *They will not hurt nor destroy in all my holy mountain;*

for the earth will be full of the knowledge of Yahweh,

as the waters cover the sea.

(Above) He is wisdom, justice, and the advocate for the down trodden. He is the bringer of peace and under His rule all violence will cease. Everyone will be safe extending even to the animal world. This is important because one of the four horseman was given a power to kill humans through animals. When Jesus comes into His Kingdom and destroys Babylon along with its power, animals will no longer be predators or eat flesh. This alone is an amazing witness to the judgment the Father released on the earth. Originally, the animals lived in harmony with man and each other, even in the time of Noah. However, ever since the judgment was released soon after the flood animals have become violent and predators according to the judgment. Animals have been a danger to man killing many.

These are the four winds of God's judgment: (1) Death by evil men of conquest and domination, (2) wild animals, (3) famine (4) plagues (sickness, and natural disasters). However, when Babylon is destroyed, so is the powers which were released with it. There will be a returning to harmony with the animals both with man and with each other. Death by the animal kingdom and within it is proof that we are now and have been living under God's judgment against the world. However, this state will not last forever.

3) NIV Rev 5:6 *Then I saw a Lamb, looking as if it had been slain . . . He had seven horns and seven eyes, which are the seven spirits of God sent out into all the earth.*

The third manifestation is that of the suffering servant, or the sacrificial Lamb of God.

NIV Isa 52:13 *See, my servant will act wisely;*
he will be raised and lifted up and highly exalted.
NIV Isa 52:14 *Just as there were many who were appalled at him—*
his appearance was so disfigured beyond that of any man
and his form marred beyond human likeness—
NIV Isa 52:15 *so will he sprinkle many nations,*
and kings will shut their mouths because of him.
For what they were not told, they will see,
and what they have not heard, they will understand.

WEB Isa 53:1 *. . . To whom has the arm of Yahweh been revealed?*
WEB Isa 53:2 *For he grew up before him as a tender plant,*
and as a root out of dry ground.
He has no good looks or majesty.
When we see him, there is no beauty that we should desire him.
WEB Isa 53:3 *He was despised,*
and rejected by men;
a man of suffering,
and acquainted with disease.
He was despised as one from whom men hide their face;
and we didn't respect him.
WEB Isa 53:4 *Surely he has borne our sickness,*
and carried our suffering;
yet we considered him plagued,
struck by God, and afflicted.
WEB Isa 53:5 *But he was pierced for our transgressions.*
He was crushed for our iniquities.
The punishment that brought our peace was on him;
and by his wounds we are healed.
WEB Isa 53:6 *All we like sheep have gone astray.*
Everyone has turned to his own way;

and Yahweh has laid on him the iniquity of us all.

WEB Isa 53:7 He was oppressed,

yet when he was afflicted he didn't open his mouth.

As a lamb that is led to the slaughter,

and as a sheep that before its shearers is silent,

so he didn't open his mouth.

WEB Isa 53:8 He was taken away by oppression and judgment;

and as for his generation,

who considered that he was cut off out of the land of the living

and stricken for the disobedience of my people?

WEB Isa 53:9 They made his grave with the wicked,

and with a rich man in his death;

although he had done no violence,

nor was any deceit in his mouth.

WEB Isa 53:10 Yet it pleased Yahweh to bruise him.

He has caused him to suffer.

When you make his soul an offering for sin,

he will see his offspring.

He will prolong his days,

and Yahweh's pleasure will prosper in his hand.

WEB Isa 53:11 After the suffering of his soul,

he will see the light and be satisfied.

My righteous servant will justify many by the knowledge of himself;

and he will bear their iniquities.

WEB Isa 53:12 Therefore will I give him a portion with the great,

and he will divide the plunder with the strong;

because he poured out his soul to death,

and was counted with the transgressors;

yet he bore the sin of many,

and made intercession for the transgressors.

Isaiah describes well the manifestation of Christ as the suffering servant—the lamb with its throat cut. All of which He endured in order to create and save His beloved.

NIV Rev 5:7 He came and took the scroll from the right hand of him who sat on the throne.

NIV Rev 5:8 And when he had taken it, the four living creatures and the twenty-four elders fell down before the Lamb. Each one had a harp and they were holding golden bowls full of incense, which are the prayers of the saints.

NIV Rev 5:9 And they sang a new song:

"You are worthy (equal to, deserving) to take the scroll

and to open its seals,

because you were slain,

and with your blood you purchased men for God

from every tribe and language and people and nation.

NIV Rev 5:10 You have made them to be a kingdom and priests to serve our God,

and they will reign on the earth."

NIV Rev 5:11 Then I looked and heard the voice of many angels, numbering thousands upon thousands, and ten thousand times ten thousand. They encircled the throne and the living creatures and the elders.

With His blood He purchased men for God . . .

Amp Rev 5:10 And You have made them a kingdom (royal race) and priests to our God, and they shall reign [as kings] over the earth!

Jesus has made for Himself an entire nation, a Kingdom, a race of celestial humans which will live in the New Jerusalem and rule the mortal humans on the natural earth with Him.

Now in verse 11 (above) angels numbering thousands upon thousands, and ten thousands, times ten thousand are added to the scene of those before the throne.

WEB Rev 5:12 saying with a loud voice, "Worthy is the Lamb who has been killed to receive the power, wealth, wisdom, strength, honor, glory, and blessing!" 13 I heard every created thing which is in heaven, on the earth, under the earth, on the sea, and everything in them, saying, "To him who sits on the throne, and to the Lamb be the blessing, the honor, the glory, and the dominion, forever and ever! Amen!" 14 The four living creatures said, "Amen!" The elders fell down and worshiped.

In the beginning of this heavenly scene in Rev 4:8-12, the Father was revealed and was worshiped as He had taken His place on the throne. He carried with Him His complete plan to bring a conclusion to the old corrupted creation, and the blueprint of a whole new creation. It is a complete plan having been worked out by the Father within the restrictions of the promise which binds His throne with a rainbow. That promise being to not conclude human history and the earth with a destroying flood. Now, He is glad to turn over to His Son this plan for Him to not only reveal to both the heavens and the earth these plans, but for Him to implement them. This is why there is a gathering before the throne and a shift of worship in Rev 5:12 towards the Son by whom the blueprint can be revealed and carried out! This is a defining moment in all of creation! Judgment has been issued by the Father, the verdict is announced and executed by His Christ and Son!

What is the contents of the scroll with its seven seals? The contents of the scroll is the complete plan or blueprint for the new heavens, the new earth, and the New Jerusalem with its celestial humans (the perfected souls of the elect). These plans will come into being only after the close of the corrupted old plan of creation takes place. The seven seals are the events or the sevenness of which is to take place in order to fully conclude the old plan of creation. This includes the enforcement of the justice of all things corrupted, and the salvaging of those from the old creation who would inherit this future. The plans for the new heavens and the new earth are sealed up and unable to be implemented until that which binds it closed has been completed, which is the sevenness of judgment and redemption. The scroll is the good news of the Gospel.

Some may say about the judgment of fire, what's the difference between wiping out the earth with a flood and wiping out the earth with fire?

NIV Ge 9:8 Then God said to Noah and to his sons with him:

NIV Ge 9:9 "I now establish my covenant with you and with your descendants after you

NIV Ge 9:10 and with every living creature that was with you—the birds, the livestock and all the wild animals, all those that came out of the ark with you—every living creature on earth.

NIV Ge 9:11 I establish my covenant with you: Never again will all life be cut off by the waters of a flood; never again will there be a flood to destroy the earth."

NIV Ge 9:12 *And God said, "This is the sign of the covenant I am making between me and you and every living creature with you, a covenant for all generations to come:*
NIV Ge 9:13 *I have set my rainbow in the clouds, and it will be the sign of the covenant between me and the earth.*
NIV Ge 9:14 <u>Whenever I bring clouds over the earth and the rainbow appears in the clouds,</u>
NIV Ge 9:15 <u>I will remember my covenant between me and you and all living creatures of every kind. Never again will the waters become a flood to destroy all life.</u>
NIV Ge 9:16 *Whenever the rainbow appears in the clouds, I will see it and remember the everlasting covenant between God and all living creatures of every kind on the earth."*
NIV Ge 9:17 *So God said to Noah, "This is the sign of the covenant I have established between me and all life on the earth."*

There is a school of thought that asserts that it did not rain before the flood. According to Scriptures a mist or morning dew would rise up from the earth to water the plants each morning. The topography and ecology of the earth changed tremendously as a result of the flood. Especially the amount of water which now lays on the surface of the earth. If rain did not happen before the flood or was a rare event, and considering the trauma of the flood struck fear in the hearts of men afterwards, this promise God made about not destroying the earth with a flood is paramount towards the peace of men. Without that promise, every time it would rain all of man would go into a panicky frenzy thinking life was over, that another flood has started. Even with this promise men were frightened. It is one of the primary reasons the tower of Babel was built.

However, given all the changes and the amount of water which afterwards lays on the surface of the earth, rain became the main way the earth is watered. A cycle of evaporated water due to the sun, now collects in the sky and falls back to the earth when it become too heavy. That cycle is a normal part of the ecology we know today. But it was not considered normal for them in the days following the flood until they had become accustomed to it. As such and back then, for them to see it start raining might be synonymous with the end of the world. God was being kind to give us a promise and a sign that told us not to fear the life giving waters which fall to the earth. When it rained and the rainbow would come out, one could be at ease and joyful that the earth had been watered. Likewise, and because they have that promise by God, we can let our guard down and not be afraid that even though this time it stopped, one day it might not stop, and doom the earth. By the promise of God we no longer had to fear the most essential life sustaining element there is in the earth—water.

Likewise, to again destroy the earth that way would be to destroy all life on it. Especially since the last time only 8 and a handful of animals survived starting life over again in the aftermath. This is the first difference of one from the other method of judgment.

Although the earth and mortal man is judged a second time as unredeemable, unlike the first judgment, it will happen in an instant, with a thunderous crash melting every element of the universe with fire. Humanity will become extinct as will the universe its habitat is comprised of. Although 8 humans survived the flood and repopulated the world, with this second judgment, humanity or natural humans become extinct. However, in keeping His promise never to wipeout all life with a flood, through the redeeming work of Jesus numbers of humans beyond counting are metamorphized into a new species of humans. They become celestial humans with embodiments which have as their natural habitat the spiritual realm, and no longer the natural realm of the physical universe. There is no vessel like the ark which any number of humans can survive the coming destruction of the earth, as the ark provided for the 8. There is only one way. That way is to be born again becoming a celestial human, the way provided by Christ. Yes, there is only one way!

God is not content to just trashing the old creation and all in it because it became corrupted. In His order things must have proper and just closure, and every promise kept. He must give time to repay good for evil suffered and evil for those who were evil. All the books must be balanced out before it is finished. Those who were cheated and robbed of what God had given them will be repaid. Those who had ill-gotten gain through covetousness and jealousy will have loss and punishment to even the score.

So again, the seals which are the bindings of this scroll keep the contents from coming into being. Until they are broken or fully loosed and their purposes served, they will continue to seal the new heavens and earth from the beginning. That makes the seals the planned conclusion to end the old creation. Whereas the scroll is the plan and blueprint for the new creation to follow. In the history of history can there be a more significant and spectacular event to witness than to be in the court of heaven while this decision (verdict) is revealed and its meaning made known?

Note:

- **There are two creations**, the first is the seven days of creation in the book of Genesis, the one we live in which is judged for destruction. The second, the new heavens and the new earth, is the one written in the scroll which is to come, which is created for eternity in the spiritual realm, not in the natural realm as the first.
- **There are two Adams.** The first Adam and the last Adam.
- **There are two judgments**, the first was by water, the flood. The second is by fire.
- **There are two lines of offspring.** The first is the line of offspring of Eve's, the woman clothed with the sun. Those whose spirit makes God their Father by possessing the Spirit of Christ—the Spirit of the bride. The second is the line of offspring of the Devil, whose spirit father is the Devil, and they possess the corrupted human spirit of Adam and Eve.
- **There are two deaths**, the first is a natural death. The second is a death by being thrown alive into the lake of fire for eternity.
- **There are two lives**, the first is our natural life. The second is when we receive our celestial bodies transcending from being a natural human to a celestial human.
- **There are two resurrections of the dead**. The first are those who were martyred for their testimony during the great tribulation and will rise to reign with Christ during His millennium reign (this resurrection will not face the judgment or the second death). The second resurrection is of all the dead who will be sorted out as sheep or goats and face eternal life or a second death in the lake of fire.
- **There are two raptures.** The first is for those who are in *spiritual union* with Christ who will be lifted from the earth as the Holy Spirit departs the

earth; leaving the world in a complete desolation and subject to the kingdom of darkness with no restraints (the great tribulation). The second rapture, will happen for the elect who participate in the first resurrection as well as those who are alive at the first resurrection and have not taken the mark of the beast nor have they worshipped the image of the beast and who have stood fast on their testimony of Jesus.

- **There are two dwellings for the dead, the disembodied.** The first is Hades, which is temporary and all will come out of it to be resurrected when its time is finished. The second is the lake of fire which is eternal and those who will be thrown alive into it will have had first endured the disembodiment in Hades.

- **There are two eternal destinations.** The first is the new heavens and the new earth in the spiritual realm. The second is the lake of fire.

CHAPTER 4

The First Four Seals

*WEB Rev 6:1 I saw that the Lamb opened **one of** (the first of) **the seven seals**, and I heard one of the four living creatures saying, as with a voice of thunder, "Come and see!" 2 And behold, a white horse, and he who sat on it had a bow. A crown was given to him, and he came out conquering, and to conquer. 3 When he opened **the second seal**, I heard the second living creature saying, "Come!" 4 Another came out, a (fiery) red horse. To him who sat on it was given power to take peace from the earth (power to war), and that they should kill one another. There was given to him a great sword. 5 When he opened **the third seal**, I heard the third living creature saying, "Come and see!" And behold, a black horse, and he who sat on it had a balance (scales) in his hand. 6 I heard a voice in the middle of the four living creatures saying, "A choenix (a quart or one loaf of wheat bread) of wheat for a denarius, and three choenix (quarts or three loafs of barley bread) of barley for a denarius! Don't damage the oil and the wine!" 7 When he opened **the fourth seal**, I heard the fourth living creature saying, "Come and see!"*

NLT Rev 6:8a And I looked up and saw a horse whose color was pale green like a corpse. Amp Rev 6:8b [black and blue as if made so by bruising],and its rider's name was Death, and Hades (the realm of the dead) followed him closely. And they were given authority and power over a fourth part of the earth to kill with the sword and with famine and with plague (pestilence, disease) and with wild beasts of the earth.

The first four of the seven seals releases the four horsemen also known as the four horsemen of the apocalypse. These four horsemen are the comprehensiveness of evil which are the powers behind the Devil and the beast with their respective seven heads (kings and kingdoms) in Revelation. The four horses the angels of destruction ride, represent the powers the angels have been granted.

The fourth horse called, "Death" is like the seventh seal in that the seventh seal contains the seven trumpets of God's wrath against the world—a seven within a seven. The seven trumpets are the sevenness of the means that the seventh seal is carried out through. The fourth horse named, Death, contains the four different forms or means of death and destruction of that pale green horse—a four within a four. These four means of death and destruction of the fourth horse (listed below), are the four winds of God's destruction, and are the means the other three horses accomplish their purposes.

NIV Jer 49:35 *This is what the LORD Almighty says: "See, I will break the bow of Elam, the mainstay of their might.*
NIV Jer 49:36 *I will bring against Elam the four winds from the four quarters of the heavens*
NIV Eze 14:21 *"For this is what the Sovereign LORD says: How much worse will it be when I send against Jerusalem my four dreadful judgments—sword and famine and wild beasts and plague—to kill its men and their animals!*

The sword, famine, wild beast and plague (disease, and natural disasters) are the four means that death is able to prematurely take an ongoing 1/4 or 25% of the world's population before their time. This (fourness of) comprehensive destruction was released at the beginning of the seven ages of the beast. That is a few generations after the new beginning, after the flood in answer to Nimrod's rebellion.

The name, "the four winds," gives the image of wind sweeping across the globe from the four points of the compass. They are comprehensive and all inclusive affecting everything, working their way through all time from the beginning of the seven ages of evil, to the end of the ages. They are like yeast working its way through an entire batch of dough as they work their evil throughout the entire globe.

They were released soon after the new beginning, just a few generations after the flood. However, they have been restrained and not allowed to have full expression of their power until the end and global rule by the lawless one is achieved (namely, the human counterpart of the first angel and his white horse). They have been frustrated and limited in the conquest, domination of the world, enslavement, and the destruction they were allowed to accomplish until this global expression is achieved in the last three and a half years before their punishment comes. Although granted and released by God according to His judgment, these elements of evil power were called down by the magic and incantations of the one man who was looking for ultimate power, domination, and conquest.

Amp Rev 18:23 . . . *by your magic spells and poisonous charm* (sorceries) *all nations were led astray* (seduced and deluded).

That one man is Nimrod, also known in the Bible as "the Assyrian", Amraphel, the man of lawlessness, the beast, and the antichrist.

Many fables exist concerning Nimrod and extra biblical sources give him a fearsome reputation. The Targum says, Nimrod became a mighty man of sin, a murderer of innocent men, and a rebel before the Lord. In Arabic literature Nimrod is considered as the supreme example of the tyrant (al-jabbar). Nimrod was supposedly the originator of sun worship and founder of Babylon which became the ancient centre of Baal worship and occult practices of every kind including demon worship, sacrificing children to demons, black magic, séances, miraculous materializations, witchcraft, astrology and sorcery (all of which are condemned in the Bible).

The Rabbinical literature identifies Nimrod with Cush and Amraphel meaning 'he whose words are dark'. He is described as the first hunter, subsequently becoming carnivorous and introducing meat eating to others, and he was the first man to make war against other peoples. Nimrod's identity is linked with Gilgamesh and it is said that he persecuted Abraham. According to this source he is responsible for the Tower of Babel.

The Apocryphal Book of Jasher gives a lot of detail describing Nimrod as an idolater and rebel against the Lord. Here he is called a mighty hunter who fought battles of his brethren against all their enemies *(the false messiah or better known as the antichrist)*. The curse of Noah had apparently taken effect since the sons of Canaan were in the power of the sons of Noah's son Japheth. Nimrod came against the sons of Japheth and conquered them.[1]

It is with him, Nimrod, that man's defiance against the judgment of God begins. He was born just a couple of generations after the flood. Nimrod was saying to God, I will not submit to you or your order! I will fight you and I would rather die fighting than to accept the lot in life you gave me. However, this is not just Nimrod's sin, the people made Nimrod king over them, while wanting to go the way of Nimrod, and defy God.

Because he was victorious in battle against the Japhethites, Nimrod was like a shark who tasted blood and went into a feeding frenzy. He decided to take his life into his own hands apart from God. To not only defy God but to fight Him. Through his victory he decided to take what he willed and to be free of God's authority and to do as he pleased, to gain his own happiness apart from God. Rebellion became his way.

He discovered how humans made their own rules and gained their own happiness before the flood. He was now angry and against God for destroying his descendents in the flood, and wanted to do anything which would bring back the conditions of the world before the flood.

Note: It is one thing to sin against God, but a whole new realm of rebellion opened up to defy God and refuse His discipline. Even Cain did not do this after murdering his brother and God condemned him. Cain accepted his lot and asked for mercy, which was given by a mark to protect him in his exile. Conversely, Nimrod threw off his chains and boundaries God had disciplined his lineage with, and in stark defiance fought against God and His people deciding he would not only refuse his fate God had assigned his lineage to, but would fearlessly and boldly fight God to the death in rebellion. I would rather die than be subordinated and conform to your will, in so many words was his creed. This afterwards earned him so much awe and adoration from his fellow men that they took his example by following him and made him king over the whole earth. For no one had ever conceived of doing such a thing nor did they believe they could succeed in defying God until Nimrod. It is at this time when everyone made Nimrod king over themselves that God released the second judgment of fire on the world starting with the four horsemen.

Since then it has not been the best of humanity and its lineage who has had authority and rules the earth, but Nimrod—Babylon—the ones who lust for domination, conquest, and power. The worst and most disrespectful of authority and of fellow human beings are those who have ruled the globe. It is the judgment and punishment of God against the people of the earth to be suppressed by this defiance they embrace. As the old saying goes, be careful what you ask for, you just might get it. As this study goes on we will see how relevant to the plan of judgment and redemption this defiance and rebellion to be self-determined actually is. It is central.

> As a result of this victory Nimrod was the first person to wear a crown and be called a king: And when Nimrod had joyfully returned from battle, after having conquered his enemies, all his brethren . . . assembled to make him king over them, and they placed the regal crown upon his head. According to this source Nimrod started well but became wicked and did not follow the ways of the Lord becoming more wicked than all his predecessors from the flood onwards. And he made gods of wood and stone, and he bowed down to them, and he rebelled against the Lord, and taught all his subjects and the people of the earth his wicked ways. (Book of Jasher Chapter 7)

Flavius Josephus the Jewish Historian wrote in his 'Antiquities of the Jews':

Now it was Nimrod who excited them to such an affront and contempt of God. He was the grandson of Ham, the son of Noah, a bold man, and of great strength of hand. He persuaded them not to ascribe it to God, as if it were through his means they were happy, but to believe that it was their own courage which procured that happiness.

He also gradually changed the government into tyranny, seeing no other way of turning men from the fear of God, but to bring them into a constant dependence on his power... Now the multitude were very ready to follow the determination of Nimrod and to esteem it a piece of cowardice to submit to God; and they built a tower, neither sparing any pains, nor being in any degree negligent about the work: and, by reason of the multitude of hands employed in it, it grew very high, sooner than anyone could expect; but the thickness of it was so great, and it was so strongly built, that thereby its great height seemed, upon the view, to be less than it really was. It was built of burnt brick, cemented together with mortar, made of bitumen *(tar)*, that it might not be liable to admit water.............

These words resonate so clearly today. There is contempt for the God of the Bible combined with a dramatic growth in the occult; political correctness insidiously dictates; people rely on everything and anything rather than God and ascribe nothing to God; many consider it cowardice to submit to God; many do not spare any pains in building their own kingdoms (or towers). This is not only sad but very dangerous. Antichrist not only means against Christ but in place of Christ, he is an imitator and a master deceiver making the false look genuine. .... they exchanged the truth about God for a lie and worshiped and served the creature rather than the Creator who is blessed forever! Amen.(Romans 1/25) [1]

An early Arabic work known as Kitab al-Magall or the Book of Rolls (part of Clenentine [a Christian Church Father] literature) states that Nimrod "saw in the sky a piece of black cloth and a crown; he called Sasan the weaver to his presence, and commanded him to make him a crown like it; and he set jewels in it and wore it. He was the first king who wore a crown. For this reason people who knew nothing about it, said that a crown came down to him from heaven." Later, the book describes how Nimrod established fire worship and idolatry, then receives instruction in divination for 3 years from Bouniter[2]

We will learn more about him later. However, when we look at the first horseman we see:

WEB Rev 6:2 ... *A crown was given to him, and he came out conquering, and to conquer.*

We see how this verse (above) coincides with Nimrod's vision, from heaven he was given a crown. He was the first ruler to have one, he was declared the king of the world by the people of his day, he also was the first king of Babylon and its founder/builder. As a part of God's judgment on mankind (above) the first decree was to give the tyrant a crown to dominate and conquer. Jesus, on the other hand, ushered in His Kingdom by taking a crown of thorns (a crown of suffering) and being a sacrificial lamb instead of a tyrant king of domination. In every way, Jesus is the complete opposite of the antichrist.

Here (below) are the four powers or authorities Nimrod called down through his magic, and God granted as a part of His judgment. Take note how they are progressive in scope and when combined they give the possessor of these powers total lordship and command of all life on the earth. Meaning, when he comes into the fullness of his power every life on earth will serve him, and through death he can cut short any life at will. Truly this is a condemning judgment loosed by God against man:

1) A white horse: ". . .behold, a white horse, and he who sat on it had a bow. A crown was given to him, and he came out conquering, and to conquer." A crown (authority) of power of conquest to conquer. The white horse is a power to rule—it is a sovereignty. This power is unlimited in scope, for it was granted that this crown would rule the entire earth. The only limitation is its timing. It will take until the end times before the fullness of this power can be achieved by the Devil and the one man it was granted. However, since it was released a couple of generations after the flood, it has been restrained from attaining global domination until God permits it.

NIV 2Th 2:7 For the secret power of lawlessness is already at work; but the one who now holds it back will continue to do so till he is taken out of the way.
NIV 2Th 2:8 And then the lawless one will be revealed, whom the Lord Jesus will overthrow with the breath of his mouth and destroy by the splendor of his coming.
NIV 2Th 2:9 The coming of the lawless one will be in accordance with the work of Satan displayed in all kinds of counterfeit miracles, signs and wonders,
NIV 2Th 2:10 and in every sort of evil that deceives those who are perishing. They perish because they refused to love the truth and so be saved.
NIV 2Th 2:11 For this reason God sends them a powerful delusion so that they will believe the lie

NIV 2Th 2:12 and so that all will be condemned who have not believed the truth but have delighted in wickedness.

When it is no longer restrained the amount of time he will have that rule without interference has been decreed and limited to three and a half years. In this study we call it the kingdom of darkness. Which is the time of the great tribulation. When it's time is over, Jesus too will then come on a white horse which is (for Him) a power to rule the whole earth for not three and a half years, but for one thousand years. He returns as the King of kings, the ruler of all that was created in the heavens and the earth, even over life and death does His authority reign.

2) A fiery red horse: "Another came out, a (fiery) red horse. To him who sat on it was given power to take peace from the earth (power to war), and that they should kill one another. There was given to him a great sword." An authority of power (ability) to gather men into huge armies to war. The white horse before it, has a power of conquest and to impose rule and dominate. Although, God has granted a power to rule the whole earth, it is something it's possessor must take and impose by his own force through his lust and greed for power. The first judgment on the earth and its inhabitants was one of water, through the flood. Through this power of attaining domination through war, the judgment of fire on the earth has its beginning. In the end, all the elements of the natural universe melt in a fire, and finally all is thrown into the lake of fire. Then the judgment of fire will have had its end.

3) A black horse: "and he who sat on it had a balance *(scales)* in his hand." This is a power and authority to lord over the world, to impose tyrannical powers and a justice system which results in its enslavement. The power of the black horse is the power of bondage and servitude. This rider's authority is over the world finances (riches) and commodities, he also has a power to enslave the captives of his rule and conquest, pressing the objects of his rule and conquest into service and hard labor. This is how Nimrod built his many great cities. In the beginning slave labor was used to build Babylon, Nineveh, Egypt and so on. We know by the records in the Bible of the account of the Israelites in Egypt of how slave laborers were reduced to livestock status. The wages of their labor while in service to the beast, barely earned them enough food to live on.

4) A pale green horse: A power and authority to kill by different means sending its disembodied victims to the realm of the dead—Hades. With a power to kill the first horse or crown of authority has the ultimate and needed consequence to impose his force.

NIV Eze 14:21 "... *my* (the Lord's) *four dreadful judgments—sword and famine and wild beasts and plague—to kill its men and their animals!...*"

The four dreadful judgments of the Lord are mentioned many times by the prophets and Moses. Then once more by John in Revelation.

Note: It is interesting that one of the favorite means to kill Christians and Israelites alike was to feed them to wild animals to be mauled and torn apart, even while an audience entertained itself by the horror of this spectacle. It is also speculated that the elite in the new world order have a strategy of taking advantage of war, famine, sickness, and natural disasters (plagues) to further their cause in depopulating the world. It is because these men of power are given their power from the spirit of Babylon.

It's important to note about this last horse and rider that it was said it was given the limit of only being able to kill a quarter of mankind. Starting when this judgment was released and ending when its power is broken by the return of Jesus Christ, this horse and rider is able to take an ongoing 25% of the world's population. Violence (including war), famine, plagues (including sickness and natural disasters), and predatorial beasts have been bringing premature death to one out of every fourth person in the world in each generation since this judgment was released soon after the flood. As long as humans are being born, one out of every four are doomed to die prematurely from one of these four dreadful means. I guess the good news is, it can't go beyond those numbers (for now).

What this means is, when an ongoing fourth of the population is not being consumed by sickness, disasters of nature, famine, or death by wild animals, it is inevitable that a war will break out. This is so death may take its due of one out of every four humans born out of the population. Likewise, if we were at peace then famine will break out. If the world food supply was adequate for the entire population of the world, it is inevitable that natural disasters and disease will make up the difference so that one out of every four humans born on this earth will meet an untimely and premature end.

This is an irrefutable judgment and a power given to the Devil. As long as predatorial beasts have been killing man; as long as disease has been taking lives; as long as starvation has plagued the earth; as long as organized violence, war, enslavement, and empirical rule have put the world in bondage from the time of the first king, is exactly how long this judgment has been in effect. During that time it has been oppressing, stealing the peace of mankind, and taking an ongoing one fourth of the world's population. This has been since a couple of generations after the flood. We live in a hostile, condemned and unfixable world which has a curse on it.

It is a futile idea to think that we could feed the entire world, keep it safe from the wild animals and natural disasters, eliminating all of the illnesses, and bringing war and violence to an end by forming a one world government. It is the doom of man to forever fight against injustice, find cures, and struggle to feed the world. It is only the delays of God which have given us temporary victories in those four areas. However, we must open our eyes, our victories against the plagues of man are only delaying the inevitable. It is a false sense of having control because God has granted, according to His judgment against the inhabitants of the earth, that one out of every four humans born will come to a premature death—no more, but more importantly, no less. Amen! The power of man can do nothing to change this. This a terrible and sobering truth of the state of this corrupt world we live in. It is not a toss of the dice that so many die in the earth, but it is an executed judgment by God and a curse on man.

This is the proper understanding of the condition of man and of the evil in the world. We all have a choice, we can serve God, or serve ourselves. Serve God and we step into freedom and out of the authority of the Devil, his antichrist, and their power over the whole earth which is the power of the four horsemen. The second choice is to serve self, and suffer being placed under the judgment of God by being put under the power and authority of the Devil, his antichrist, and their power of the four horsemen.

This is the power Nimrod asked for through his magic, and it was the choice of the men of the earth to put themselves under the Devil and Nimrod while becoming free from God. And it was the judgment of God to grant it, "so be it!" Again, choose to serve yourself and it is the curse and judgment against man for him to have to fight the whole of his life against oppression and forced servitude, starvation, sickness and calamities (natural disasters). Choose to serve God and these judgments and curses and powers have no authority over you.

Amp Ro 6:18 *And having been set free from sin, you have become the servants* (slaves) *of righteousness (of conformity to the divine will in thought, purpose, and action).*

Amp Ro 6:19 *I am speaking in familiar human terms because of your natural limitations. For as you yielded your bodily members [and faculties] as servants* (slaves) *to impurity and ever increasing lawlessness, so now yield your bodily members [and faculties] once for all as servants* (slaves) *to righteousness (right being and doing) [which leads] to sanctification.*

Amp Ro 6:20 *For when you were slaves of sin, you were free in regard to righteousness.*

Amp Ro 6:21 *But then what benefit (return) did you get from the things of which you are now ashamed? [None] for the end of those things is death.*

Amp Ro 6:22 *But now since you have been set free from sin and have become the slaves of God, you have your present reward in holiness and its end is eternal life.*

Amp Ro 6:23 *For the wages which sin pays is death, but the [bountiful] free gift of God is eternal life through (in union with) Jesus Christ our Lord.*

This terrible judgment God has given, is one that man asked for and continues to ask for when they prove they want to live life independently and serve themselves.

We are so lost we see our state of independence from the authority of God as normal. It is true in that God is granting the wicked, the objects of His wrath what they want, domination, and for everything to serve them. However, to the objects of His mercy who in their spirit think it is freedom to be independent from God and able to do as they will, He doesn't wipe them out, but sentences them to forced servitude. They are enslaved by the world and then like Jesus, who is the way, they learn obedience through suffering. According to this judgment they are forced to stop living for self and to live for another's pleasure. For those who would live eternally their life experience would help them have a different outlook on life.

This is why when God blessed Abraham with many descendants who have the promise of the world to come, He told Abraham that when their number increased (to a certain population) they will be slaves for 400 years. To qualify for the world to come, we must have a heart of servitude towards God and not an independence from Him or a will to do as we please. Every time His people would lose the right heart, God would give them over to enslavement again and again in order to break their willful pride to serve self. All done so they might remain the people of the promise.

These four seals release the four horsemen. They are released simultaneously a couple generations after the flood in judgment of the rebellion of Nimrod and of the people of the earth who made him king over them. They desired to defy God and do as they please, as Nimrod had shown them how to do. Compounding that, they were looking for the pre-flood ways of tearing down the boundaries between the natural and the supernatural in order to gain personal power to dominate and empower themselves with.

What do these curses mean to humanity? By way of justice and punishment, God gave the world what it asked for. He has decreed by the white horse that a single man bent with a spirit of conquest and domination can; through the red horse make war, rob the earth of its peace putting men against each other while allowing ultimate and eventual victory to the one man. In giving that man victory and domination over the world God granted him through the black horse to enslave his subjects, enriching himself and his elite by giving him control over the resources and commodities of the earth. Lastly allowing him to impose his own tyrannical laws and justice, because men have rebelled and refuse the laws and justice of God.

By way of God's justice and punishment, He gives leave that all this could happen and be enforced through the pale green horse called death. God allows death to consume a fourth of mankind; to take an ongoing 25% of the world's population prematurely before their time. God calls the four means He granted death to take its due, the four winds of His destruction. They are; 1) the sword (violence) 2) wild beast 3) famine, and 4) plague (disease and natural disasters). The first wind of destruction turns man against man, the last three makes nature turn hostile against man. It is to Hades that death gives its disembodied souls to be confined until the day of judgment, when they will rise to life and face the second death. Life resembled nothing like this after the flood until the rebellion of Nimrod and the people of the earth provoked God to judge the world a second time.

It is only Jesus and when He returns that we will be set free from these curses. Once again, it will be a time when men, animals, and nature will be in harmony and in mutual support of each other. When Jesus was on the earth He once said:

GNT Jn 6:26 *Jesus answered, "I am telling you the truth: you are looking for me because you ate the bread and had all you wanted, not because you understood my miracles. 27 Do not work for food that spoils; instead, work for the food that lasts for eternal life.*

This is an interesting statement by Jesus. Often it is not the answers which are the most important, but the right questions. Questions which put us on the right track of thinking. By what Jesus said, we can know there is something significant about His miracles that we should question, or ponder, other than the fact that He could upon demand miraculously feed and satisfy our bellies.

To figure it out we need first to question the types of miracles Jesus performed. The people He was addressing numbered around 5,000 and they were excited to follow Him because He had fed them when there was no food to do so. After having fed them He had walked on the water and rebuked a storm, which immediately was quieted and became calm. The people He fed followed Him and wondered how He had gotten where He was when there were no boats to travel in. It is then Jesus made this statement about not understanding the significance of His miracles to those who followed Him. In addition, Jesus was known for routinely healing the sick and dying, even freed the people from tormenting spirits, and demons. He raised people from the dead. He turned water into wine. He restored the ear of a man who had it severed off with a sword. Death and Hades could not hold Him. He Himself rose from the dead.

The miracles Jesus performed unequivocally testified to the fact that Jesus had an authority over that of the four horsemen and the four winds of destruction: The sword (violence and war), famine (starvation), plague (disease and natural disasters), and death by the wild beasts of the earth. When death came and Hades scooped up

His disembodied soul, it could not hold Him, but three days later He rose from the dead. In addition, He set free 144,000 of those who were held captive in Hades. When Jesus returns to rule His Kingdom it says:

NIV Isa 11:6 The wolf will live with the lamb, the leopard will lie down with the goat, the calf and the lion and the yearling together; and a little child will lead them.
NIV Isa 11:7 The cow will feed with the bear, their young will lie down together, and the lion will eat straw like the ox.
NIV Isa 11:8 The infant will play near the hole of the cobra, and the young child put his hand into the viper's nest.
NIV Isa 11:9 They will neither harm nor destroy

It is by the judgment of God that we live under these four winds of destruction, and the four horsemen! It is the beginning of the judgment of fire that the world is under and has already been loosed.

NLT Jn 3:16 "For God so loved the world that he gave his only Son, so that everyone who believes in him will not perish but have eternal life.
NLT Jn 3:17 God did not send his Son into the world to condemn it, but to save it.

He did not send His Son into the world to condemn it but to save it. How is that the case? Because the world has already been judged! The first four seals which were released simultaneously was the beginning of the sentence of being condemned after the gavel of judgment having gone down. The fifth seal is God sending His Son to save those who are already under that judgment and sentence. The walking dead on death role who are unable to escape their doom of being condemned to suffer two deaths are given by the very Judge who sentenced them a pardon, if they accept.

*NLT Jn 3:18 "There is no judgment awaiting those who trust him. **But those who do not trust him have already been judged** for not believing in the only Son of God.*
NLT Jn 3:19 Their judgment is based on this fact: The light from heaven came into the world, but they loved the darkness more than the light, for their actions were evil.
NLT Jn 3:20 They hate the light because they want to sin in the darkness. They stay away from the light for fear their sins will be exposed and they will be punished.

NLT Jn 3:21 But those who do what is right come to the light gladly, so everyone can see that they are doing what God wants."

We see further evidence of this truth as well as a greater understanding of it (below):

Amp Jn 9:35 Jesus heard that they had put him out, and meeting him He said, <u>Do you believe in and adhere to the Son of Man or the Son of God?</u>
Amp Jn 9:36 He answered, Who is He, Sir? Tell me, that I may believe in and adhere to Him.
Amp Jn 9:37 Jesus said to him, You have seen Him; [in fact] He is talking to you right now.
Amp Jn 9:38 He called out, Lord, <u>I believe! [I rely on, I trust, I cleave to You!] And he worshiped Him.</u>

Despite his expulsion from the temple by its leaders for trusting Jesus, this former blind man decides to believe Jesus is from God and then binds (cleaves) himself to Jesus through trust in and obedience (worship) to Him. Thus, he becomes reconciled to God.

Amp Jn 9:39 Then Jesus said, <u>I came into this world for</u> (or, because of) <u>judgment [as a Separator, in order that there may be separation between those who believe on Me and those who reject Me], to make the sightless</u> (or the naive to their own sin) <u>see and to make those who see become blind.</u>
Amp Jn 9:40 Some Pharisees who were near, hearing this remark, said to Him, <u>Are we also blind?</u>
Amp Jn 9:41 Jesus said to them, If you were blind, <u>you would have no sin</u> (or better said; your sin would not be counted against you)<u>; but because you now claim to have sight, your sin remains. [If you were blind, you would not be</u> (held) <u>guilty of sin; but because you insist, We do see clearly, you are unable to escape your guilt.]</u> (judgment and its ensuing sentence)

In other words, since you say you know the difference and still reject me, then you have made your choice and you have decided to remain in your sin continuing to reject God—remaining in defiance and rebellion towards Him. I will, therefore, give you over to your own arrogant self-deception and sin because you pridefully will not open yourself up to the truth of your real condition and relationship with God. I will make you, (who say you see [know the truth] but do not, and are not open to it) even more blind. You prideful fools! I will let you be and remain subject to the doom looming over your head which has already been loosed upon you!

In His judgment, God is sympathetic to those who are naive to their own sin and rebellion against God, even though we all are, nevertheless, guilty and deserving of His judgment and sentence. This is not unlike the Church of the end times of which He says, you are "lukewarm", "neither hot or cold." And, because of this condition "I am about to vomit you out of my mouth (divorce, disown, disconnect from my union with you)." However, and unlike the end times Church, God wants to give benefit of doubt. The whole of mankind has been judged a second and final time. Although we all are guilty and all are under the sentence already loosed in the world, God has sent His Son to those who would reconcile with God through Him—those who would believe, adhere, and obey Him. The Son then saves them who are willing from the doom they (ignorant or not) have already been given over too. Humanity itself in its entirety is doomed for extinction!

When it says those who believe will be saved, it actually means that those who believe this is true: That the whole world has already been judged and condemned. In addition, believing that humanity is living on borrowed time and there is only one way out: That is by becoming a celestial human through union with Jesus. Nonbelievers think this is a fabricated story. They don't believe humanity has been judged and can't believe they personally have been judged thinking they are a basically good person. However, this knowledge of being under judgment already implemented is the information the Father gave to the Son to give to His bride, His followers. That information is revealed on that scroll. No other in heaven or on earth has been given that knowledge, nor have they been found worthy of it.

There is no power of man's which can overcome the four horsemen and the four winds of destruction! Make advances medically to curb disease, and famine will break out. Feed the world and war will break out. Bring peace then nature, animals including insects, and natural disasters will take the due Death and Hades has been given authority to have. It is the curse of man to struggle at consoling, comforting, aiding and saving each other from these four winds of destruction. Nevertheless, death will have its 25% one way or another and feed Hades which will imprison the souls of the disembodied. It is not by faith, but by historical record that Jesus has already shown us through the miracles He routinely performed that it is Him alone who can save us from being swallowed up in death and imprisoned by Hades. It is He who can save us from being subject to the four horsemen, and the four winds of destruction! The price: To reconcile yourself with God by forsaking your very essence of awareness, the human spirit, in preference to perceiving, living, and being moved by God's own Spirit—the Spirit of Christ.

Notes

[1] Gisborn, T. (n.d.). *Nimrod the Worlds First Tyrant and Forerunner of the Antichrist.* Retrieved October 2012, from Hubpages: http://eliora.hubpages.com/hub/NIMROD-THE-WORLDS-FIRST-TYRANT-AND-FORERUNNER-OF-THE-ANTICHRIST

[2] *Nimrod.* (2013, December 3). Retrieved October 2012, from Wikipedia, The Free Encyclopedia: http://en.wikipedia.org/wiki/Nimrod

CHAPTER 5

The Fifth Seal

*WEB Rev 6:9 When he opened **the fifth seal**, I saw underneath the altar the souls of those who had been killed for the Word of God, and for the testimony of the Lamb which they had.*

The fifth seal is the redemption of God amidst His judgment. It is here at the fifth seal that Jesus becomes the sacrificial Lamb of God. He is killed on the cross and goes to Hades then raises from the dead. Afterwards, He ascends to heaven to be seated at the right hand of His Father. However, when coming before His Father after His ordeal and as like the train of His robe flowing gracefully behind Him, He presents the "first fruits" of His redeeming work to His Father. He has "spread His tent over them (Rev 7:15)." These "souls" underneath the altar who were killed for the Word of God are the 144,000. They are the first to be redeemed—the first fruits! They are from among the disembodied souls in Hades—the dead. They are the first to become celestial humans, receiving celestial bodies.

NIV Rev 6:11 "Then each of them was given a white robe"

These disembodied souls who were killed were given celestial bodies (white robes). Again, they are the first fruits of the redeeming work Jesus had done on the earth. They are the line of offspring of the woman clothed with the sun and the moon under her feet with the crown of 12 stars upon her head. Below are three more occasions which tell us about the fifth seal and the resulting redeeming work it initially accomplished in the 144,000.

NAS REV 7:1 *After this I saw four angels standing at the four corners of the earth, holding back the four winds of the earth, so that no wind would blow on the earth or on the sea or on any tree.*

NAS REV 7:2 *And I saw another angel ascending from the rising of the sun, having the seal of the living God; and he cried out with a loud voice to the four angels to whom it was granted to harm the earth and the sea,*

NAS REV 7:3 *saying, "Do not harm the earth or the sea or the trees until we have sealed the bond-servants of our God on their foreheads."*

NAS REV 7:4 *And I heard the number of those who were sealed, one hundred and forty-four thousand sealed from every tribe of the sons of Israel:*

The above verses refers to the judgment of the four horsemen and the four corresponding winds of destruction which bring premature death to the inhabitants of the earth. They are restrained by the angels of the Lord until a mark of God is given to the 144,000 so that loosed judgment cannot stop God's planned redemption. Again, so that the four winds of destruction cannot stop the 144,000 from fulfilling their role in God's redemption.

NIV Rev 14:1 *Then I looked, and there before me was the Lamb, standing on Mount Zion, and with him 144,000 who had his name and his Father's name written on their foreheads.*

This verse (above) is referring to Jesus having suffered the cross as the sacrificial Lamb, and the first fruits of His salvation that are gathered to Him. They are identified here as the 144,000. Likewise, in Rev 14:4 (below) they are identified as the first fruits of the redeemed. Mathew 27:50 (below) confirms it as true:

NIV Mt 27:50 *And when Jesus had cried out again in a loud voice, he gave up his spirit.*

NIV Mt 27:51 *At that moment the curtain of the temple was torn in two from top to bottom. The earth shook and the rocks split.*

NIV Mt 27:52 *The tombs broke open and the bodies of many holy people who had died were raised to life.*

NIV Mt 27:53 *They came out of the tombs, and after Jesus' resurrection they went into the holy city and appeared to many people.*

NIV Mt 27:54 *When the centurion and those with him who were guarding Jesus saw the earthquake and all that had happened, they were terrified, and exclaimed, "Surely he was the Son of God!"*

These patriarchs or "holy people" referred to in verse 52 (above) are obviously the first fruits of the redeeming work Jesus accomplished on the cross by virtue that they were set free from death immediately after Jesus breathed His last. The 144,000 are said to be the first fruits which identifies them as the "many holy people" who were raised to life leaving their tombs.

NIV Rev 14:2 And I heard a sound from heaven like the roar of rushing waters and like a loud peal of thunder. The sound I heard was like that of harpists playing their harps.
NIV Rev 14:3 And they sang a new song before the throne and before the four living creatures and the elders. No one could learn the song except the 144,000 who had been redeemed from the earth.

These 144,000 who are now the first to become celestial humans are the only ones who can learn this song of redemption and sing it to Him who sits upon His throne, the one who saved them. None will be added to their numbers or learn the song until the murder of Stephen. However, from Stephen forward up until the great tribulation, neither Stephen or his Christian brothers have needed to wait disembodied in Hades to be rescued. Starting with Stephen, Jesus keeps His promise that they will in no way taste death, but go from life to life. They receive their celestial body while in audience in front of the throne of God and His Son before the head of their natural body hits the ground in death.

NIV Rev 14:4 These are those who did not defile themselves with women, for they kept themselves pure. They follow the Lamb wherever he goes. They were purchased from among men and offered as firstfruits to God and the Lamb.
NIV Rev 14:5 No lie was found in their mouths; they are blameless.

"They did not defile themselves with women" refers to the fact that they kept their DNA pure from Noah and Abraham forward to the Christ. Noah's DNA was pure going back to Seth. The seed of Eve (the Christ) starts from the line of offspring of Seth, her son. The 144,000, 12,000 from every tribe, are the righteous Israelites who are the 12 stars of Eve's crown through which Jesus was born. This line of offspring who kept their DNA pure have a special place in the heart of Jesus. Through them He was able to come in the flesh to save the human race.

WEB Rev 6:10 *They cried with a loud voice, saying, "How long, Master, the holy and true, until you judge and avenge our blood on those who dwell on the earth?" [11] A white robe was given to each of them. They were told that they should rest yet for a while, until their fellow servants and their brothers, who would also be killed even as they were, should complete their course.*

Although they have been redeemed and saved from being disembodied and confined in Hades by being given celestial bodies, they are being told they have to wait for justice against those who had them killed. When will that be? When the wicked have finished serving the purposes of God. That will be at the end of the great tribulation. It is then that God's promise is to avenge their blood and that of their fellow servants—their brothers—will He destroy their murderers. God has counted the 144,000 souls, who were the first fruits of His redeeming work, as one with those who are to be killed during the great tribulation. They will be the disembodied souls who will lose their lives for the sake of their testimony of Jesus during the great tribulation. They too will be raised from the dead, then given celestial bodies in the same manner as the 144,000 were. This future event John calls, "the first resurrection" (Rev 20:4-6).

The fifth seal helps us understand the promise of God that at the end of the ages their prayers will be answered from all the ages, but for now (at this time in the vision) it is allowed to go on. However, what this tells us is where in the history of mankind the fifth seal happens and what it represents. The fifth seal is when Jesus died on the cross and rose from the dead. It represents the release of the redemption of God after having released His sentence of judgment through the first four seals.

Note: This order enlightens us about something very important. That is referring to judgment and condemnation being released first, then salvation being released second. It seems God has learned a lot through the flood. Noah preached for 100 years that a flood was coming and no one believed him. Then, he sealed up the ark with the 7 others as the rest of mankind mocked them. However, when the flood was well in progress those on the outside clawed at the doors and begged Noah to let them in.

Releasing the seals in this order on this occasion of the second judgment, it is like God having Noah build the ark after it started raining and after the waters are well in progress, then open up the door for people to be rescued before they drowned. Judgment had begun with the four horsemen—it has already started to rain. It is after that He releases His redemption (the fifth seal) and affords for us to be rescued before the flood waters of the second judgment kill everyone!

Another important thing to note concerning the 144,000: When they asked God to avenge their blood on those who dwell on the earth, they knew the earth had just rejected the Father's Son and had killed Him too, just as they had done to them because of their testimony of God. Jesus had just joined their numbers in being martyred. When they say, "avenge our blood..." they are including Jesus' blood as part of "our blood" because he had just been killed too. It stands to reason this is what occasioned their feeling of, "enough is enough!" Then appealed to the Father their request. It's like, what more can they do to prove they hate God and deserve to burn in hell? They have had it, because now the world killed the Lord of Glory and they see no more reason to delay or to tolerate the evil in the world! However, God answers them by saying, that "they should rest yet for a while, until their fellow servants and their brothers, who would also be killed even as they were, should complete their course."

They too did not understand how God was using the evil in the earth not only as judgment but also as a means to save and purify the elect. They were focused on the world's total violence and rejection of God. It is this event in heaven where John is watching this all take place that it is being revealed why God's plan is allowing this to go on and why He is taking these measures to bring the history of creation to a close. God desires that all be saved from the destruction of the human race. It is out of mercy, love, and patience to save all who would be saved, and not out of tolerance or complacency of evil that God concludes His creation and the natural human race.

CHAPTER 6

The Sixth Seal

WEB Rev 6:12a *I saw when he opened **the sixth seal**, and there was a great earthquake.*

This earthquake happens after the last seven years of the 70-7's has been completed. It is a marker that signifies the start of the global desolation decreed by God during which the great tribulation happens. 30 days after the end of the 70th-7 the false prophet enters the temple and creates an image of the beast who is the antichrist, the eighth and final king of Babylon (having formerly been the founder of Babylon and the first of its seven kings), Nimrod. The abomination which causes desolation is what the false prophet will create in making an image of the beast, then give life to the image so that the disembodied soul of Nimrod can raise from the dead out of the Abyss, and embody himself with that image (as granted by God).

NLT Da 9:27 *He will make a treaty with the people for a period of one set of seven, but after half this time, he will put an end to the sacrifices and offerings. Then as a climax to all his terrible deeds, he will set up a sacrilegious object (an abomination) that causes desecration (desolation), until the end that has been decreed is poured out on this defiler, (the desolater)."*

NIV Da 12:11 *"From the time that the daily sacrifice is abolished and the abomination that causes desolation is set up, there will be 1,290 days.*

3-1/2 years or 1,260 days after the midpoint of the last 7 marks the end of the 70-7 year periods. 1,290 days after the midpoint or 30 days after the end of the 70-7's is when the end comes, starting with the false prophet creating an image of the beast. It is not a statue as most would assume. It is important to take note that the Bible, the Lord, and Daniel are very careful to not refer to the creation of this "image" as a person, or a human being. The Bible calls this person and his recreated body, "the beast." Jesus calls the risen beast alive in the created body of the false prophet, an "abomination," as in, an abomination of nature. As such, Daniel calls his recreated body an image of the beast instead of the recreated body for the beast.

NIV Rev 17:8 The beast, which you saw, once was, now is not, and will come up out of the Abyss and go to his destruction. The inhabitants of the earth whose names have not been written in the book of life from the creation of the world will be astonished when they see the beast, because he once was, now is not, and yet will come.

On the last day, the Lord will call everyone ever born out of Hades, the realm of the dead, the disembodied souls who have died. He will clothe them for a second time giving them all a resurrected body in which to face the throne of God and be judged. Make no mistake, the body Nimrod receives when he rises up out of the Abyss is not a body of God's making. The body which Nimrod returns from the dead and occupies is something which is made by man.

This body the false prophet creates for the disembodied soul of Nimrod could perhaps be from the mixture of celestial and human DNA creating a giant which caused the judgment which brought on the flood. Or perhaps the body parts of other humans who were sacrificed in the temple by the false prophet were obtained in order to make this body (image), as was done in the fictional account of Frankenstein.

NIV Rev 13:15 He (the false prophet) *was given power to give breath to the image of the first beast, so that it could speak and cause all who refused to worship the image to be killed.*

Whatever is the case it is an image or replica of the body of Nimrod who currently is a disembodied soul confined in the Abyss. The false prophet is granted the power to give the breath of life to it and it becomes the body that Nimrod, can reside in. Nimrod escapes death because of the magic of the false prophet. To add insult to injury, he does this abominable thing in the temple of God.

NIV Rev 17:17 For God has put it into their hearts to accomplish his purpose <u>by agreeing to give</u> <u>the beast their power to rule, until God's words are fulfilled.</u>

A desolation is the absence of the presence of God. The Jews had suffered that condition more than once in their history. These occasions were facilitated by the Spirit presence of God abandoning the temple, or God turning His face and favor away from them. In second Chronicles 7:12-22, the Lord gives instruction to King Solomon on how to end a desolation and regain His attention, intervention, and His Spirit presence back in the temple after it is withdrawn. However, God's Spirit is in the earth during these contemporary times no longer in the stone temple built by men in Jerusalem, but in the hearts and bodies of those Christians who are in union with Christ. No longer residing in a stone temple but in living temples of flesh. No longer in a fixed location on top of the temple's foundation, is the Spirit of God in the earth, but in every corner of the globe walking and talking, having expression everywhere through those He is in union with and who obey and then carry out His promptings.

As a result, when the Spirit presence of God is removed it is not a local event in Jerusalem as it was in the past, but a global event. By God withdrawing from the earth evacuating the two witnesses, His Spirit, and those in whom He occupies their bodies, evil breaks free of the shackles of restraint that the Holy Spirit's presence in the earth imposes. Intervention by God will cease for 3-1/2 years. Man will be on his own and whatever will happen will happen.

NIV Rev 13:10 If anyone is to go into captivity, into captivity he will go. If anyone is to be killed with the sword, with the sword he will be killed.
This calls for patient endurance and faithfulness on the part of the saints.

The proper question at this time is why did the false prophet do such an abominable thing in the temple of God by making an image, a body, for Nimrod through which his soul could live again? Likewise, why did the people of the earth beg the false prophet to do so? The answer is because of their desire to be saved from the two witnesses of God who were stifling the efforts of the people desiring independence from God.

The affairs of man have come full circle! It was Nimrod who originally incited the people to live independent from God and His authority so that they could live by their own power and be free to do as they will. The people made Nimrod king over them because he promised to kill God, and protect the people from God's consequences so they could do as they pleased. It was this betrayal and decision by the people of the earth which caused God to judge the world a second time. However, not with a flood as before, rather this time with fire. Everything will eventually be destroyed and thrown into the lake of fire making natural humans and the entire universe extinct.

Now, after the 70-7's, the false prophet is bringing Nimrod back from the dead with the promise that he will again (supposedly) save the world from God and specifically from the two witnesses who have proven to be unkillable. The world is making the same mistake that Sodom and Gomorrah made. Only this time it is not the folly of two cities and a handful of suburbs, but the entire globe.

Note: Like the assumption that the image the false prophet creates is a statue, here is another false assumption. The men of Sodom and Gomorrah and the surrounding suburbs were not assaulting the house of Lot in order to have homosexual sex motivated by unbridled lust with the two angels Lot was protecting. The truth is that they were looking to create a giant of their own by somehow joining in union with the angels who were manifest in visible human form, mixing celestial and human DNA. As it was accomplished in the days leading up to the flood.

The reason why, was that previously their cities and towns had been raided and pillaged by an army led by a giant they were helpless to defend against. That giant was Nimrod who (supposedly) could not be defeated in combat. However, in an effort to recover the women, stores, and wealth of his nephew Lot who resided in one of those cities, Abraham met Nimrod and his army in battle. It was by the power of God that Abraham overcame and recovered all that was taken from the two cities and their surrounding towns. He returned everything to them and refused to be enriched or rewarded by them for what he had done. As a result and in answer to the destruction suffered by the giant Nimrod, the kings and citizens of these cities and towns did not turn to the God of Abraham who had just saved them. In their own power they instead decided to do as was done which brought on the flood.

They unanimously agreed to make a giant of their own by mixing the DNA of humans with that of celestial beings. This way, according to their own thinking they could better protect their cities and towns with their created giant. Just as the people of the world will encourage the false prophet to do in bringing back the beast and giant Nimrod in order to save them from the two witnesses of God.

As a result of their determination and pursuit, the Lord then visited Abraham who God had helped the people of Sodom and Gomorrah through. He informed His friend that He was about to destroy the cities Abraham had helped protect and restore. The Lord had made His decision to destroy them because of their choice and activities to make a giant. This was an abominable course of action which had in the past led to God destroying the entire world with a flood. Abraham could not fathom that it was everyone who was choosing this evil course of action.

Because of the intercession of Abraham, the Lord relented and sent His two angels who were manifest in human form. Before destroying them He showed Abraham the resolve of all the people except Lot to abuse these manifest angels in order to create their giant. All the men of both cities and their surrounding villages went to Lot's home where the angels were being hosted in order to overpower the angels so they could carry out their evil intentions. Abraham now saw that except his nephew Lot who protected the angels, the people of those cities unanimously were bent on this pre-flood evil and that it was every one of them who gathered together in strength to overcome the angels. It was just as in the days of Noah who was the only man who had not been corrupted with evil. It was likewise that all of the people made Nimrod king over them to rebel against God and do as they pleased.

With fire and brimstone (burning sulfur) God destroyed these cities and all who were in them, annihilating them utterly. However, because of the intercession of Abraham, the righteous that were in those cities and did not agree to help overpower the angels to carry out that evil, were saved from its destruction. Sadly, as with Noah it was only one man, Lot, who was against their plans, and tried to protect the angels. And as with Noah, Lot and his family were saved from the ensuing destruction. It will be the same when the false prophet raises the giant Nimrod back from the dead so the two witnesses of God can be killed. It will be because of the intercession of Jesus, this time, that God will save from the globe those in His Church who are in union with Him. Those who will be saved will be against the trend of the whole world who support the false prophet in recreating the giant Nimrod to save them from the two witnesses. They will be "caught up," raptured and rescued like Noah and Lot, removed from the globe so they will not be harmed or suffer the winds of God's judgment and destruction. When the end comes and the Lord catches up those who are in union with Him, it will have been unanimously among the people for the two witnesses of God to be stopped at all costs.

In wanting the unkillable killed just as with Sodom and Gomorrah the people of the world commission the false prophet to create a body for the disembodied giant, Nimrod, to come up from out of the Abyss and rule the people in rebellion to God. However, this is no longer on a local level like the cities of Sodom and Gomorrah, but on a global scale involving the whole world. The Lord punished Sodom and Gomorrah in a way to warn us of the penalty of committing such an abomination in the eyes of the Lord. It is the lake of fire and brimstone for the whole earth when they go the way of Sodom and Gomorrah and the pre-flood days by bringing back the giant or demigod Nimrod. Peter warned about this very thing but the world does not take heed:

NIV 2Pe 2:4 For if God did not spare angels when they sinned (by mixing their DNA with natural women creating giants), *but sent them to hell* (the abyss), *putting them into gloomy dungeons to be held for judgment;*
NIV 2Pe 2:5 if he did not spare the ancient world when he brought the flood on its ungodly people, but protected Noah, a preacher of righteousness, and seven others;
NIV 2Pe 2:6 if he condemned the cities of Sodom and Gomorrah by burning them to ashes, and made them an example of what is going to happen to the ungodly;
NIV 2Pe 2:7 and if he rescued Lot, a righteous man, who was distressed by the filthy lives of lawless men
NIV 2Pe 2:8 (for that righteous man, living among them day after day, was tormented in his righteous soul by the lawless deeds he saw and heard)—
NIV 2Pe 2:9 if this is so, then the Lord knows how to rescue godly men (by evacuating them entirely away from planet earth) *from trials* (the great tribulation) *and to hold the unrighteous for the day of judgment, while continuing their punishment.*

Again, in verse 9 Peter specifically is pointing out by the record that God can save His bride, those in union with Him, from the great tribulation that is coming on the whole world. God is able to save the godly as He did for Noah from a global flood, and Lot from the fire and brimstone of the second judgment. Likewise, He will do the same for those who are in union with Christ, by rescuing them with the rapture before the great tribulation.

That earthquake of the sixth seal is a result of the Holy Spirit withdrawing from the earth, taking with Him the two witnesses and the *Church Pure* with a "snatching up" of them. The earthquake marks when the rapture happens and judgment on the *Church Corrupt* begins. Revelation 11:3-13 gives more details of this event:

NIV Rev 11:3 *And I will give power to my two witnesses, and they will prophesy for 1,260 days, clothed in sackcloth."*

NIV Rev 11:7 *Now when they have finished their testimony, the beast that comes up from the Abyss will attack them, and overpower and kill them.*

NIV Rev 11:11 *But after the three and a half days a breath of life from God entered them, and they stood on their feet, and terror struck those who saw them.*

NIV Rev 11:12 *Then they heard a loud voice from heaven saying to them, "Come up here." And they went up to heaven in a cloud, while their enemies looked on.*

NIV Rev 11:13 *At that very hour there was a severe earthquake and a tenth of the city collapsed. Seven thousand people were killed in the earthquake, and the survivors were terrified and gave glory to the God of heaven.*

That earthquake in verse 13 is the earthquake of the sixth seal.

WEB Rev 6:12b *The sun became black as sackcloth made of* (goat) *hair . . .*

The sun turned black like sackcloth made of goat hair represents God's Spirit presence being withdrawn from the earth, creating total spiritual darkness. This happens at the rapture when the Holy Spirit withdraws and lasts for 3-1/2 years. The next or seventh seal, which is released simultaneously with the sixth, makes reference to this time of global desolation known also as the great tribulation when it says:

NAS Rev 8:1 *WHEN HE [the Lamb] broke open the seventh seal, there was silence for about half an hour in heaven.*

In this case, one hour represents the "hour of power" granted the beast to rule the earth unrestrained by God. It is a cycle of time which in this case is a week of years, or 7 years. That "hour of power" begins with the withdrawal of the Holy Spirit, the two witnesses, and the *Church Pure* from the earth and ends with the battle of Armageddon. It follows that for heaven to be silent for "half an hour" it is telling us that heaven, or God, will be inactive and not present in the earth for 3-1/2 years. That is the 3-1/2 years of the great tribulation which is the time of global desolation.

However, after the desolation and eventually during the second half of that hour of power, the kingdom of the beast is plunged into total darkness. There will be no sun, moon, or stars to illuminate the earth. The sun becoming black like sackcloth has a literal meaning as well. When Jesus comes into His Kingdom and defeats the army of Babylon at Armageddon, the earth will thereafter rely on the light of the Lord to spill over the walls of the New Jerusalem and illuminate the entire earth.

"As sackcloth made of goat hair. . ." On the last day the goats will be separated from the sheep. The sheep will be given eternal life and those considered goats will suffer a second death by being thrown alive into the lake of fire. The spiritual darkness that will overtake the earth is brought on by the darkness of the goats in the world.

> **An early Arabic work known as Kitab al-Magall or the Book of Rolls (part of Clementine [A Christian Church Father] literature) states:** that Nimrod "saw in the sky a piece of black cloth and a crown; he called Sasan the weaver to his presence, and commanded him to make him a crown like it; and he set jewels in it and wore it. He was the first king who wore a crown. For this reason people who knew nothing about it, said that a crown came down to him from heaven." [3]

This sackcloth that blots out the light of the world made of goat hair is like the black cloth that was in the sky that Nimrod saw in his vision that also brought with it a crown for him. In both cases, the black cloth represented the spiritual darkness that would overtake the world when the antichrist comes into his power. Which in Nimrod's vision, is him.

Conversely, Jesus calls Himself the light of the world. Below are a few verses which reference that:

WEB Jn 8:12 Again, therefore, Jesus spoke to them, saying, "I am the light of the world. He who follows me will not walk in the darkness, but will have the light of life."

In this verse (above) Jesus is actually referencing the time of darkness to come (both the spiritual and natural darkness). The light that comes from within Him will indeed save us from that time, and will in the end be the light which illuminates the earth. That is why Jesus says of Himself, "I am the light of the world (Jn 9:5)." It is literal and will happen when He comes into His Kingdom and after the sun will lighten the earth no more.

WEB Jn 12:35 Jesus therefore said to them, "Yet a little while the light is with you. Walk while you have the light, that darkness doesn't overtake you. He who walks in the darkness doesn't know where he is going. 36 While you have the light, believe in the light, that you may become children of light."

Jesus is warning that He is in the earth to save for only a short time longer. As long as He is here in the body and afterwards remaining in the bodies of believers in Spirit. The people of the world have an open invitation to become "children of the light." He is here to save the walking dead. For the verdict has already been decided, and the sentence has already been set in motion—the human race is already condemned!

WEB Jn 12:46 I have come as a light into the world, that whoever believes in me may not remain in the darkness.

WEB Jn 9:4 I must work the works of him who sent me, while it is day. The night is coming, when no one can work. 5 While I am in the world (whether in the flesh or in the Spirit), I am the light of the world."

WEB Rev 6:12c . . . and the whole moon became as blood.

The whole moon turned blood red represents the blood of the elect being martyred during this time of spiritual darkness. The moon is a heavenly body which reflects the light of the sun and is a light in the darkness. The Church reflects the light of Jesus in this darkened world as the moon is light for the night. Since it is utterly destroyed, the Church (moon) turns red from the blood which is spilled in it—the whole Church is destroyed.

> WEB Rev 6:13 *The stars of the sky fell to the earth, like a fig tree dropping its unripe figs when it is shaken by a great wind.*

"The stars falling from the sky like figs drop from a fig tree when shaken by a great wind" is reference to the those who the Lord calls "the elect" who are being slain in massive numbers during the great tribulation by the antichrist and his 10 kings of the earth who are without restraint. One of the main reasons they are also called stars in the heavens, is because stars are, again, light in the darkness. Likewise, stars have celestial or heavenly stature just as the elect do. Not only that, but they are guiding lights in the darkness. Stars are used to navigate by. In Daniel, it says of those who will understand the end times and teach others to understand, they are like stars who shine—they illuminate in the darkness (Da 12-3). One final comparison is that the stars are in the heavens just as the Spirit power of those who are called shining stars on the earth.

" . . . like figs drop from a fig tree when shaken by a great wind . . ." The tree is the *Church Corrupt*, the Catholic Church, and those churches who have gone their way. The figs are the fruit of those Churches, the elect within them. The great wind which shakes the tree causing the figs to fall (die) are the winds of God's destruction.

> WEB Rev 6:14 *The sky was removed like a scroll when it is rolled up. Every mountain and island were moved out of their places.*

It is a richly symbolic description in Revelation 6:12-13 of the natural and spiritual devastation which happens during the great tribulation as carried out by human agents (the beast and his 10 kings of the world). At this point in the book of Revelation starting with verse 14 (above) the global desolation known as the great tribulation has run the course of its time. The "half an hour" out of the "hour of power" (42 months) the beast was granted no restraint imposed by heaven above is concluded.

Heaven had been silent, or inactive, for 3-1/2 years. In that hour of power God has given the people of the earth a taste of what they have been praying for and calling down upon themselves throughout time, since the whole world made Nimrod king over them. The full number of the fellow servants and brothers of the 144,000 who have been killed has become complete. It is time for the promised justice from God against those who killed the elect. Now, at the middle of that hour of power, heaven is no longer silent. God's wrath begins when the sky literally recedes like a scroll.

Note: After the great tribulation is forced to end by God from then on out it is the agents of heaven which carry out the wrath of God against those who destroyed the Church and killed the elect. The heavenly host had stood still in silence waiting for their turn while the Church suffered at the hands of the world. It will be cosmic events and natural disasters which will be administered by angels, followed by monstrous creatures loosed from out of the Abyss which will torment and kill the enemies of God. As such, there will be no mistaking that the plagues which are suffered are judgments from God.

Secondly, as we go forward in interpreting from this point we should lean more to the literal side than the symbolic. The stars falling from the heavens (the spiritual realm) from this point forward will be angels and not the elect who have heavenly stature. That is because their time of suffering is finished. The elect who remain alive on earth will now receive a mark of God which will protect them from harm. In other words, no more will die because God had put an end to the great tribulation. They will be protected until the day of the first resurrection. Sometime after their brothers who had perished during the great tribulation raise from the dead, they will together raise up into the sky as celestial humans to join Jesus in His descent to earth.

Amp 1Th 4:16 For the Lord Himself will descend from heaven with a loud cry of summons, with the shout of an archangel, and with the blast of the trumpet of God. And <u>those who have departed this life in Christ will rise first.</u>
Amp 1Th 4:17 <u>Then we, the living ones who remain [on the earth], shall simultaneously be caught up along with [the resurrected dead] in the clouds to meet the Lord in the air; and so always (through the eternity of the eternities) we shall be with the Lord!</u>

Included in the descent to the natural earth will be Jesus and His Father, the New Jerusalem, the angels of the Lord, those who have died and have already received their celestial bodies, those who die in the great tribulation and have need to be resurrected (because of the desolation of that time). This is the first resurrection.

Finally, those who are alive and survive the great tribulation will rise up in the sky and join them.

Note: In regards to those resurrected in the first resurrection and those caught up in the sky with them who survive the great tribulation, it is only these two groups of people who qualify to participate in these two events (the first resurrection and being caught up receiving a celestial body). They qualify by first having suffered the great tribulation. Secondly, by not coming off their testimony of Christ, not worshiping the beast, and not receiving his mark.

The opening of the sixth seal starts with the great tribulation and is marked by a huge earthquake. It then goes on to give us what marks the end of the great tribulation, when not a single of the elect will be killed ever again. That mark is the sky rolling up like a scroll—the sign of the Son of Man. However, the first resurrection and the ensuing rapture (of being "caught up") will not occur for a little shy of 3-1/2 additional years. Although the living elect will have a mark of God on them and cannot be harmed, the earth will be pure hell to live on during this time. Their relief and salvation comes at the first resurrection, and that will happen in the days before the seventh trumpet of the seventh seal sounds.

Amp Rev 10:7 But that when the days come <u>when the trumpet call of the seventh angel is about to be sounded, then God's mystery (His secret design, His hidden purpose), as He had announced the glad tidings to His servants the prophets, should be fulfilled (accomplished, completed).</u>

God's mystery:

NIV Lk 8:10 He said, "<u>The knowledge of the secrets of the kingdom of God</u> has been given to you, but to others I speak in parables, so that, " 'though seeing, they may not see; though hearing, they may not understand.'

The mystery of God is His plan for the salvation of man which God foretold through His prophets and through the good news of the Gospel. The good news of the Gospel is the coming of the Kingdom of the Lord on the earth. In fact, that was the Gospel message, "The Kingdom of God is near!"

NIV Mk 1:14 ... *Jesus went into Galilee, <u>proclaiming the good news of God.</u>*

NIV Mk 1:15 *"The time has come," he said. "The kingdom of God is near. Repent and believe the good news!"*

This "mystery," this spectacle is unveiled complete with the arrival of the New Jerusalem, and His entourage including His bride, the celestial humans who will rule the natural humans on the earth for a thousand years.

NLT Rev 6:14 *And the sky was rolled up like a scroll and taken away. And all of the mountains and all of the islands disappeared.*

This is a literal cosmic event. It is the sign that Jesus is coming back to the earth.

NIV Mt 24:30 *"At that time <u>the sign of the Son of Man will appear in the sky</u>, and all the nations of the earth will mourn. They will see the Son of Man coming on the clouds of the sky, with power and great glory.*

This event of the sky and the cosmos (for that matter) being taken away marks:
- The end of the great tribulation (God's wrath against the Babylonian *Church Corrupt*) which had lasted 3-1/2 years
- The beginning of 3-1/2 years of God's wrath against Babylon that controls the world, who also killed the elect.
- The sign of the coming of Christ back to the earth to begin His Kingdom, and to defeat the world government in place—the beast's Babylon.

Here in the above verse 6:14 it reads that the sky is totally "taken away." However, we learn in verses below that it happens in a couple stages.

Stage one:

NIV Rev 8:12 *The fourth angel sounded his trumpet, and a third of the sun was struck, a third of the moon, and a third of the stars, so that a third of them turned dark. A third of the day was without light, and also a third of the night.*

This verse (above) is referring to the rolling up of the sky. The sign of the Son of Man in the sky is not something that will escape anyone! It will be a spectacular event which happens on a cosmic level. Again, this is literal! So how does that really look? And what is really happening? The answer is astonishing! The natural earth which resides in the natural universe is going to be moved by God into the spiritual realm.

Have you ever sat in an automobile and suddenly you feel like the car is rolling backwards only to realize the cars surrounding you are actually slowly moving forward and you are stationary? Or perhaps the reverse of this situation, where you suddenly feel like you are rolling forward when you are supposed to be stopped, only to realize that you are stationary but the cars surrounding you are slowly moving in reverse? Well, it will be something like that for the earth. There will be a tear in the fabric of space and time and the earth including its atmosphere will be moved through that tear into the spiritual realm from its place in the natural universe. It will not move, geographically, but dimensionally.

NLT Ro 8:19 For all creation is waiting eagerly for that future day when God will reveal who his children really are (His bride of celestial humans).

NLT Ro 8:20 Against its will, everything on earth was subjected to God's curse.

NLT Ro 8:21 All creation anticipates the day when it will join God's children in glorious freedom from death and decay (during the 1,000 years Kingdom of the Lord).

NLT Ro 8:22 For we know that all creation has been groaning as in the pains of childbirth right up to the present time.

NLT Ro 8:23 And even we Christians, although we have the Holy Spirit within us as a foretaste of future glory, also groan to be released from pain and suffering. We, too, wait anxiously for that day when God will give us our full rights as his children, including the new bodies he has promised us.

NIV 1Th 5:3 While people are saying, "Peace and safety," destruction will come on them suddenly, as labor pains on a pregnant woman, and they will not escape.

NIV 1Th 5:4 But you, brothers, are not in darkness so that this day should surprise you like a thief.

In this first stage, the tear in the fabric of space and time is like the cervix of a pregnant woman in the throes of labor, opening up resulting in the baby's head crowning out of its mother's womb. The womb is the natural universe, the cervix is the tear in the fabric of space and time, or the sky rolling up like a scroll. The crowning of the baby's head from inside the mother's womb, is reflective of the earth having pushed through into the spiritual realm to the point that "A third of the day was without light, and also a third of the night."

Since this is the first stage of this event of the rolling up of the sky, it is only a portion of the earth which is crowning into the spiritual realm. As such, when one looks up into the sky as the earth rotates they will see over the course of 24 hours from horizon to horizon 8 hours of the day sky with the sun. No longer will they see 12 hours of the day sky as it did during the natural course of the earth's 24 hour cycle. As the earth continues to rotate, the observer will see next from horizon to horizon 8 hours of the night sky with the moon and the stars, and again, it will no longer last 12 hours; as was in the past. Then to complete its 24 hour rotation, it will at this stage of this event see, from horizon to horizon, 8 hours of the spiritual realm. In this realm or sky above there is no natural universe or cosmos—no sun, moon, or stars to provide light. 1/3 of the day will be gone and 1/3 of the night will be gone. Both the day sky and the night sky have given 4 hours each. That is 1/3 of its 12 hours over to a view of the spiritual realm. 1/3 of 24 hours is 8 hours. The three 8 hour views of the sky added together total 24 hours.

At this stage the whole world will see while looking in the sky, from horizon to horizon, 8 hours of the heavenly realm every 24 hours. No person on earth will escape witnessing this spectacular and absolutely fearful phenomena!

> WEB Rev 6:15 *The kings of the earth, the princes, the commanding officers, the rich, the strong, and every slave and free person, hid themselves in the caves and in the rocks of the mountains.*

If not for one particular sight, the people alive on earth would only see total darkness, it will be like gazing into the dark abyss for 8 hours of every day. They would only see light on the fringe of the horizon as the dawn of the day sky begins to appear. That one thing they will see when their part of the earth faces the spiritual realm is Jesus, together with His army angels, and His celestial humans poised to return to the earth and to conquer the kingdom of the beast. However, before we move forward (below) is stage two of this event.

Stage two:

Stage two is simply the completion of the earth and its atmosphere breaking fully into the spiritual realm and out of the natural universe. That is to a place where there are no stars and planets. The earth will lose the light of the sun and the stars and any heavenly bodies which reflect light as well. It will be cast into total darkness. Why? Because it will no longer reside in the physical universe. When the part of this process happens that the earth is fully in the spiritual realm and Jesus finally comes out of the heavens to the earth with His entourage and the city the New Jerusalem, it will be utter darkness for the mortal humans. Even the light given off from the sight of Jesus in the sky poised to return is gone because He is in the New Jerusalem on the earth.

NIV Rev 16:10 The fifth angel poured out his bowl on the throne of the beast, and his kingdom was plunged into darkness. Men gnawed their tongues in agony
NIV Rev 16:11 and cursed the God of heaven because of their pains and their sores, but they refused to repent of what they had done.

Note: The seven angels with the seven bowls of God's wrath being poured out on the earth recorded in the second of the four narratives of Revelation (16:2-21) are what is released at the corresponding blasts of the seven different trumpets (which is the seventh seal in the first narrative).

When Jesus is on the earth inside the New Jerusalem having His wedding feast before the battle of Armageddon, it is the only time and circumstances which can occasion what Jesus described in several of His teachings—that is to be in the "darkness" where there is weeping and gnashing of teeth. The place where people will grope around in utter darkness, in sorrow on the outside, and in agony tormented by manifested demonic creatures, is on the entire earth after it has shifted into the spiritual realm away from the sun and the stars which formerly gave it light. The time is when Jesus is on earth inside the walls of the New Jerusalem with His bride.

NIV Mt 8:11 I say to you that many will come from the east and the west, and will take their places at the feast with Abraham, Isaac and Jacob in the kingdom of heaven.

NIV Mt 8:12 But the subjects of the kingdom (the Jews and Israelites) <u>will be thrown outside, into the darkness, where there will be weeping and gnashing of teeth."</u>

NIV Mt 22:10 So the servants went out into the streets and gathered all the people they could find, both good and bad, and the wedding hall was filled with guests.
NIV Mt 22:11 "But when the king came in to see the guests, he noticed a man there who was not wearing wedding clothes.
NIV Mt 22:12 'Friend,' he asked, 'how did you get in here without wedding clothes?' The man was speechless.
NIV Mt 22:13 "Then the king told the attendants, 'Tie him hand and foot, <u>and throw him outside, into the darkness, where there will be weeping and gnashing of teeth.'</u>
NIV Mt 22:14 "For many are invited, but few are chosen."

NIV Mt 25:28 " 'Take the talent from him and give it to the one who has the ten talents.
NIV Mt 25:29 For everyone who has will be given more, and he will have an abundance. Whoever does not have, even what he has will be taken from him.
NIV Mt 25:30 And <u>throw that worthless servant outside, into the darkness, where there will be weeping and gnashing of teeth.'</u>

NIV Mt 25:10 "But while they were on their way to buy the oil, the bridegroom arrived. The virgins who were ready went in with him to the wedding banquet. And the door was shut.
NIV Mt 25:11 "Later the others also came. 'Sir! Sir!' <u>they said. 'Open the door for us!'</u>
NIV Mt 25:12 "But he replied, <u>'I tell you the truth, I don't know you.'</u>
NIV Mt 25:13 "Therefore keep watch, because you do not know the day or the hour.

> *WEB Rev 6:16* They told the mountains and the rocks, <u>"Fall on us, and hide us from the face of him who sits on the throne, and from the wrath of the Lamb, [17] for the great day of his wrath has come; and who is able to stand?"</u>

" . . . every mountain and island was removed from its place." The movement of the earth passing from one dimension to another is so violent that it reshapes the topography of the earth obviously leveling the cities. The earth quakes, the mountains are leveled or lowered, and islands either fall into or are covered by the sea. In fact, Jesus states below that when the fabric of space and time tears, the stars, the planets, and the galaxies quake as well.

NIV Mt 24:29 *"Immediately after the distress of those days* (those days are referring to the 3-1/2 years of the great tribulation) *"'the sun will be darkened, and the moon will not give its light; the stars will fall from the sky, and the heavenly bodies will be shaken.'*
NIV Mt 24:30 *"At that time the sign of the Son of Man will appear in the sky, and all the nations of the earth will mourn. They will see the Son of Man coming on the clouds of the sky, with power and great glory.*

We will see more details of this when we get to the seven trumpets of the seventh seal. However, there are two basic ways the wrath of God takes form. The first is devastation to the ecosystem and the nature of the earth as it is moved into the spiritual realm in preparation of the natural to interact with the supernatural. That includes Jesus, celestial humans, angels, and the New Jerusalem residing on earth and governing the natural humans.

However, before the bliss of the Kingdom of God living together with the natural, the demonic will have done the same—interact with mortal humans. As a result of the earth moving into the spiritual realm, God's second form of wrath is administered by the release of demonic spiritual forces that will torment and kill the people of the world. The Devil will be cast down and manifest on earth with his fallen angels. We will see their form and he will be viciously angry over his humiliation.

Then the Devil will release unimaginable demonic beings out of the Abyss that God has been keeping us safe from. The release of these forces are referred to as the three "woes." The first "woe" is the release of scorpion like creatures that will sting the people causing them to suffer unbearable pain for 5 months. This alone will cause people to want death because of the agony of these stings. Thus rich and poor will ask the crumbling mountains to fall upon them so they might find relief in death. The next or second "woe" is an army of supernatural creatures that will circle the globe and kill 1/3 of the earth's population. The final or third "woe" against the inhabitants of the earth is the Lord Himself coming out from behind the walls of the New Jerusalem to meet them at the battle of Armageddon. All who gather together to resist Him will die in an instant by the words that come out of His mouth.

WEB Rev 6:16 . . . *hide us from the face of him who sits on the throne, and from the wrath of the Lamb . . .*

In the backdrop of all this and before Jesus touches down on earth, the people of the earth will be terrified of the sight they see when looking up in the sky which is Jesus in the spiritual realm, poised to come down, administer justice, and conquer the kingdom of the beast—the one world government. Again, this backdrop of Jesus in the sky is the sign of the coming of the Son of Man as promised by Jesus.

144,000 Sealed

WEB Rev 7:1 After this, I saw four angels standing at the four corners of the earth, holding the four winds (the four winds of destruction) *of the earth, so that no wind would blow on the earth, or on the sea, or on any tree.* [2] *I saw another angel ascend from the sunrise, having the seal of the living God. He cried with a loud voice to the four angels to whom it was given to harm the earth and the sea,* [3] *saying, "Don't harm the earth, neither the sea, nor the trees, until we have sealed the bondservants of our God on their foreheads!"* [4] *I heard the number of those who were sealed, one hundred forty-four thousand, sealed out of every tribe of the children of Israel:*

[5] *of the tribe of Judah were sealed twelve thousand,*

of the tribe of Reuben twelve thousand,

of the tribe of Gad twelve thousand,

[6] *of the tribe of Asher twelve thousand,*

of the tribe of Naphtali twelve thousand,

of the tribe of Manasseh twelve thousand,

[7] *of the tribe of Simeon twelve thousand,*

of the tribe of Levi twelve thousand,

of the tribe of Issachar twelve thousand,

[8] *of the tribe of Zebulun twelve thousand,*

of the tribe of Joseph twelve thousand,

of the tribe of Benjamin were sealed twelve thousand.

There is a pause in the narrative between the descriptions of the sixth and seventh seals. One Bible translation correctly subtitles it as "An Interlude." That interlude is from Rev 7:1-17. There are two such interludes in this narrative. This is the first one between the end of the sixth seal and the beginning of the seventh. The second interlude which interrupts the narrative is from Rev 10:1-11:14. This second interlude lays between the end of the sixth trumpet blast and before the seventh. Both of the two interludes have two parts to them. The first interlude, wedged between the end of the sixth and beginning of the seventh seal, speaks about 1) the 144,000, and 2) the great multitude. The second interlude, wedged between the end of the sixth and the beginning of the seventh trumpet blast, speaks about 1) the angel and the little scroll and 2) the two witnesses.

The outline of Revelation dictates that the two parts of each of the two interludes have something in common with each other. The first part is the beginning of something and the second part is the end of the same thing. What that means is that the 144,000 have a thing in common with the great multitude. This makes the 144,000 the beginning of what they have in common, and the great multitude the end of what they share in common.

> WEB Rev 7:9 *After these things I looked, and behold, a great multitude, which no man could count, out of every nation and of all tribes, peoples, and languages, standing before the throne and before the Lamb, dressed in white robes, with palm branches in their hands.* WEB Rev 7:10 *They cried with a loud voice, saying, "Salvation be to our God, who sits on the throne, and to the Lamb!"* 11 *All the angels were standing around the throne, the elders, and the four living creatures; and they fell on their faces before his throne, and worshiped God,* 12 *saying, "Amen! Blessing, glory, wisdom, thanksgiving, honor, power, and might, be to our God forever and ever! Amen."* 13 *One of the elders answered, saying to me, "These who are arrayed in the white robes, who are they, and from where did they come?"*

Before it was the souls of the 144,000 who were issued white robes. Now the souls of this great multitude are too given white robes.

> WEB Rev 7:14 *I told him, "My lord, you know." He said to me, "These are those who came out of the great tribulation. They washed their robes, and made them white in the Lamb's blood.* 15 *Therefore they are before the throne of God, they serve him day and night in his temple. He who sits on the throne will spread his tabernacle over them.* 16 *They will never be hungry, neither thirsty any more; neither will the sun beat on them, nor any heat;* 17 *for the Lamb who is in the middle of the throne shepherds them, and leads them to springs of waters of life. And God will wipe away every tear from their eyes."*

What they have in common is that the 144,000 were disembodied souls who were in the paradisiacal place in Hades (under the altar), the realm of the dead. They got there by being killed for their testimony. As such, they were the first fruits of those who are redeemed, rescued from Hades, resurrected with a celestial body, and become the bride of Christ. That is taking note that their resurrection happens long before the last day.

The great multitude are those who are killed for their testimony during the great tribulation becoming disembodied souls in the paradisiacal place of Hades. As such, they are the last of those who are redeemed, rescued from Hades, resurrected with a celestial body, and become the bride of Christ. When the 144,000 asked for God to carry out justice against the people of the earth who hated God and had killed them, they were told:

NIV Rev 6:9 When he opened the fifth seal, I saw under the altar the souls of those who had been slain because of the word of God and the testimony they had maintained.
NIV Rev 6:10 They called out in a loud voice, "How long, Sovereign Lord, holy and true, until you judge the inhabitants of the earth and avenge our blood?"
NIV Rev 6:11 Then each of them was given a white robe, and they were told to wait a little longer, until the number of their fellow servants and brothers who were to be killed as they had been was completed.

The great multitude are their fellow servants and brothers who complete their numbers before the wrath of God is poured out on the kingdom of the beast. Once their numbers are complete, not a single person of God will ever be killed again. The great tribulation is over! Those who survived the great tribulation must wait until after the "first resurrection" before they are transformed into celestial humans. That being the case, the Lord will give them a mark and no harm will come to them, just as with the Jews when the plagues fell upon Pharaoh and Egypt.

When the great multitude is rescued from Hades and their disembodied state, and they become celestial humans (clean white robes), they are described as the participants of the first resurrection.

NIV Rev 20:4 I saw thrones on which were seated those who had been given authority to judge. And I saw the souls of those who had been beheaded because of their testimony for Jesus and because of the word of God. They had not worshiped the beast or his image and had not received his mark on their foreheads or their hands. They came to life and reigned with Christ a thousand years.

NIV Rev 20:5 (*The rest of the dead did not come to life until the thousand years were ended.*) <u>*This is the first resurrection.*</u>

The only thing wrong with this, one might point out, is that the 144,000 were not only the first fruits of redemption but the first by more than 2,000 years to be resurrected from the dead. Why is the Bible calling those who are killed during the great tribulation and resurrected as being the "first resurrection?" The answer is that in the mind of God, the 144,000 and the great multitude are the beginning and the end of the same event, the first resurrection even if they are separated by time. God sees from outside of time. They are a select group of souls who are to be the bride of Christ and rule with Him as celestial humans during His 1,000 year reign.

All those in between who became celestial humans, qualifying as the bride, never had to experience death right up until the rapture on the first day of the great tribulation. It will be the same for those who survive the great tribulation and qualify to be the bride of Christ. They too will never experience death but transition from their mortal body to their celestial body even before their head hits the ground in death. All others will have to wait until the last day to be resurrected.

Here is one further notation about the 144,000 and the great multitude, and why they were placed in the timeline after the sixth seal and before going on to the seventh seal. The reason is because the two groups follow in order, the 144,000 is reflected in the fifth and the great multitude is reflected in the sixth seal. After the sixth seal is broken details are given about both groups. The fifth seal concerns the 144,000 and how because of their martyrdom they became the first celestial humans (the first fruits) and the first of the bride because of their testimony. The sixth seal reveals the event which kill the great multitude (the great tribulation) and how they become celestial humans in the first resurrection. The great multitude are the last (fruits) who become the bride because of their testimony and martyrdom.

Note: It will be discussed how the two parts of the second interlude (the angel and the little scroll, and the two witnesses) are the beginning and end of the same event when we come to that part of the narrative; which is located at the end of the sixth trumpet blast and beginning of the seventh.

The literary structure and placement of these interludes both help in their interpretation and also verify the timeline of events, making the book of Revelation a very tight and well outlined piece of work. This in turn aids greatly with uncovering an interpretation that verifies itself through its order and outline.

In the case of the first interlude with the 144,000 and the great multitude it is placed after the end of the sixth seal and before the beginning of the seventh. The placement of the first interlude is fitting because we are told that the first resurrection will happen after the great tribulation; which is described in the sixth seal and in the days before the seventh trumpet blast of the seventh seal.

Notes

3 (n.d.). Kitāb Al-Magāll or The Book of the Rolls. In One of the Books of Clement. Retrieved from http://www.sacred-texts.com/chr/aa/aa2.htm

CHAPTER 7

The Seventh Seal

WEB Rev 8:1 *When he opened **the seventh seal**, there was silence in heaven for about half an hour.*

". . . about a half an hour . . ." of silence in heaven upon the opening of the seventh seal tells us that the sixth and seventh seals were opened simultaneously. This silence or inactivity was to give the beast his 42 months of unrestrained rule over the globe. The natural question is: Why then start the sixth and seventh at the same time if the actions of the seventh do not begin until after what the sixth seal accomplishes? The answer is because both the sixth and seventh seals are the beginning and the end of the same event, the pouring out of God's wrath on Babylon. The activities described in the sixth seal spill over into the seventh seal. Likewise, because the seventh seal is an account of the same event, differing only in its objective, it must start at the same time. It is just as it was for the first four seals which were opened simultaneously because collectively they were the released judgment of fire God decreed. Likewise, the sixth and seventh seals set in motion the utter destruction of the world and His plan of redemption for the humans in it.

Secondly, what is the difference between the two seals if they both are the release of the same thing, God's wrath against Babylon, the kingdom of the beast? The difference is that the beloved Church of Jesus had committed adultery on Him just as Hosea's wife Gomer did by having offspring with her lovers. The church of Rome is the seventh kingdom of the beast. Therefore, to destroy the church, is to destroy Babylon. However, His elect are in the *Church Corrupt* and the Lord does not desire to throw the baby out with the dirty bathwater (in a manner of speaking).

NAS REV 17:11 "*The beast* (Nimrod, the Assyrian) *which was and is not, is himself also an eighth and is one of the seven, and he goes to destruction.*

NAS REV 17:12 "*The ten horns which you saw are ten kings who have not yet received a kingdom, but they receive authority as kings with the beast for one hour.*

NAS REV 17:13 "*These have one purpose, and they give their power and authority to the beast.*

NAS REV 17:14 "*These will wage war against the Lamb, and the Lamb will overcome them, because He is Lord of lords and King of kings, and those who are with Him are the called and chosen and faithful.*"

After the *Church Pure* is caught up to heaven and made celestial humans (which is the wheat gathered to His barn), the Lord destroys Babylon starting with the seventh kingdom of the beast, the *Church Corrupt* (which is the harvest of the grapes).

WEB MIC 5:5 *He* (the risen Jesus) *will be our peace when the Assyrian* (the founder of the Babylonian Empire) *invades our land, and when he marches through our fortresses, then* (as such or because that is the case) *we will raise against him seven shepherds, and eight leaders of men.* [6] *They will rule the land of Assyria with the sword* (through the conquest of war), *and the land of Nimrod in its gates* (within its borders). *He* (the risen Jesus) *will deliver us from the Assyrian, when he invades our land, and when he marches within our border* (at the battle of Armageddon).

These seven shepherds (plus an eighth who is one of the seven) are the seven heads and crowns of both the Devil and of the beast. As is the case with all the seven shepherds/kings/kingdoms of the beast (Babylon), the previous one is always conquered with the sword (war) by the next kingdom in line. God had ordained it this way from the beginning! The next of the seven kings of Babylon always has to conquer the kingdom of the previous in order to come into his ordained destiny. God had ordained things this way for the express reason of impeding Babylon from gaining global domination before its time. God arranged things this way so that He may fully carryout the sevenness of His plan for the salvation of men, and that the timing of everything happens in such a way that the end or completion of all things converge on the same point at the same time—nothing left undone.

Accordingly, God accomplishes the destruction of the seventh kingdom of the beast (the *Church Corrupt*) by the sword of the eighth king of Babylon. That is so that the beast can come into his ordained destiny of being king of the entire globe. The eighth king will be the risen Nimrod (the Assyrian) who was the founder and first king of Babylon—the one who was, is not now, but will come up out of the Abyss.

However, since there is no ninth kingdom of the beast, which would destroy the eighth kingdom, it is Jesus Himself who destroys the eighth (and final global) kingdom of the beast at Armageddon, while ushering in His Kingdom of Heaven.

NIV Isa 14:24 *The LORD Almighty has sworn, "Surely, as I have planned, so it will be, and as I have purposed, so it will stand.*
NIV Isa 14:25 *I will crush (Nimrod) the Assyrian in my land; on my mountains I will trample him down. His yoke will be taken from my people, and his burden removed from their shoulders."*
NIV Isa 14:26 *This is the plan determined for the whole world; this is the hand stretched out over all nations.*
NIV Isa 14:27 *For the LORD Almighty has purposed . . .*

In keeping with how the next kingdom in line is to take the previous with the sword destroying it, Jesus meets the global army of the eighth and its king, Nimrod the beast, at the battle of Armageddon. Jesus utterly wipes out that army by the "sword of His mouth." The entire globe then becomes the Kingdom of our Lord until the extinction of natural humanity and the earth itself.

Both the sixth and seventh seals are released simultaneously because they are together phase one and two of the destruction of Babylon. The sixth seal's main focus is the destruction of the seventh kingdom of the beast which is the *Church Corrupt*, and the time of the great tribulation. The seventh seal is focused on the destruction of the eighth kingdom of the beast which is the risen Nimrod and his 10 kings who under him rule the globe. The seventh kingdom of the beast, the *Church Corrupt* is destroyed by the eighth kingdom of the beast. The eighth kingdom of the beast is destroyed by Jesus and His Kingdom of Heaven—the last Kingdom in the earth.

Regarding the seventh kingdom of the beast, the *Church Corrupt;* although it is utterly destroyed never to rise again from its ashes, its people are purified of their adultery with Babylon through its destruction—the great tribulation—and are therefore redeemed. They are reunited with the Lord just as Gomer was reunited with Hosea after first, her adultery, then her tribulations. The saints within the *Church Corrupt* become celestial humans and the bride of Christ—the great multitude, just as Hosea remarries Gomer. They will live and be with Jesus for eternity!

The destruction of the eighth and global kingdom of the beast does not have such a redeeming end as the seventh does. The people of the eighth kingdom are the true line of offspring of the Devil that Jesus was destined from the beginning in the garden to crush. These people have awaiting for themselves a second death to endure after the defeat at Armageddon. On the last day, 1,000 years later, they will be resurrected, clothed with a body once again, only to face judgment and be thrown alive, into the lake of fire, tormented for all of eternity!

> *WEB Rev 8:2* <u>*I saw the seven angels who stand before God, and seven trumpets were given to them.*</u> *³ Another angel came and stood over the altar, having a golden censer. Much incense was given to him, that he should add it to the prayers of all the saints on the golden altar which was before the throne. ⁴ The smoke of the incense, with the prayers of the saints, went up before God out of the angel's hand. ⁵* <u>*The angel took the censer, and he filled it with the fire of the altar, and threw it on the earth. There followed thunders, sounds, lightnings, and an earthquake.*</u> *⁶ The seven angels who had the seven trumpets prepared themselves to sound.*

After that pause for a half an hour (3-1/2 years, 42 months) heaven becomes active again. ". . . that he should add it (incense) to the prayers of all the saints on the golden altar" adding to that fire from the altar. This is in answer to the prayers of the disembodied "souls" under the altar who cried out to God for justice as a part of the fifth seal:

NIV Rev 6:9 When he opened the fifth seal, I saw under the altar the souls of those who had been slain because of the word of God and the testimony they had maintained.
NIV Rev 6:10 They called out in a loud voice, "How long, Sovereign Lord, holy and true, until you <u>*judge the inhabitants of the earth and avenge our blood?"*</u>
NIV Rev 6:11 Then each of them was given a white robe (a celestial body), *and they were told to wait a little longer,* <u>*until the number of their fellow servants and brothers who were to be killed as they had been was completed*</u>

During the "half an hour of silence" the 42 months given to the beast resulting in the great tribulation, the elect are mass murdered on what could amount to be assembly lines. It is about 3-1/2 years into the great tribulation that the full numbers of their fellow servants are met because they are killed. It is at this point that Rev 8:2-6 happens.

The censer is taken before God and He approves of the aroma which fills His nostrils. It is to Him a pleasing fragrance of those who forfeited their lives by standing on their testimony of Jesus, and refused to worship the beast or take his mark. Then He decrees it is time to answer their prayers for justice because the full numbers of those who are purified through the holding of their profession have been met.

When the angel adds the prayers of the saints crying out for justice, and fire from that altar to the incense and hurls it to the earth, this marks the end of the great tribulation. Not a single one of the elect who will be the bride will ever be killed after this—never! A mark from God is put on the survivors which prevents them from being harmed.

It says above that as a result of the censer being thrown down to the earth causes "thunders, sounds, lightnings, and an earthquake." This is the result of the tear of the fabric of space and time, causing the sky to roll back, the crinkling of space and warping of the earth as it crowns into the spiritual realm.

NLT Rev 6:14 *And the sky was rolled up like a scroll and taken away. And all of the mountains and all of the islands disappeared.*

This event is the "sign of the Son of Man's" return.

NIV Mt 24:3 *As Jesus was sitting on the Mount of Olives, the disciples came to him privately. "Tell us," they said, "when will this happen, and what will be the sign of your coming and of the end of the age?"*

NIV Mt 24:27 *For as lightning that comes from the east is visible even in the west* (visible from horizon to horizon),*so will be the coming of the Son of Man.*

NIV Mt 24:29 *"Immediately after the distress of those days* (the great tribulation) *" 'the sun will be darkened, and the moon will not give its light; the stars will fall from the sky, and the heavenly bodies will be shaken.'*

NIV Mt 24:30 *"At that time the sign of the Son of Man will appear in the sky, and all the nations of the earth will mourn. They will see the Son of Man coming on the clouds of the sky, with power and great glory.*

The tear in our physical reality exposing Jesus in the spiritual realm poised to return to the earth to subdue it, is the sign of the Son of Man. That sign is also the end of the great tribulation, and the "immediate" beginning of God's wrath poured out on the people and global kingdom of Babylon. This is what is revealed with the opening of the sixth seal. In addition, what the sixth seal describes spills over and covers what is revealed in the seventh seal, up to the fifth trumpet, which includes the first of the three "woe's." We will see the reason for this in the following, as the seven trumpets are explained.

CHAPTER 8

The Seven Trumpets

of the Seventh Seal

Now begins a new cycle of seven within a cycle of seven, the seven trumpets, which are a part of the seventh seal. It is from the standpoint of the trumpets which is the justice of God against those who hated and killed His people—the global kingdom of the beast, Babylon. This cycle of seven is the completeness and perfection, the sevenness, of God's wrath against His enemies who have now finished their usefulness to God's plan. It is His carried out plan of destruction of the line of offspring of the Devil that He promised in the garden.

God brought punishment to Nebuchadnezzar's Babylon by destroying it after their seventy years of power given to it. That had served God's plan by Babylon destroying Jerusalem and holding in captivity the Jews for seventy years. What God started after the seventy years of enslavement and promised He would complete after the 70-7's so Babylon would be destroyed utterly and forever, He now finally fulfills through the seven trumpets. All of Babylon and every place its spirit has infested, along with its every human agent in the earth, has finished its usefulness forever, and God will destroy them. However, the destruction of Babylon had started with Babylon the *Church Corrupt* and its seventh kingdom and now goes on to Babylon and its eighth and final kingdom in the world.

Note: The placement of the trumpets on the timeline is after the great tribulation, which brings an end to it.

> WEB Rev 8:6 *The seven angels who had the seven trumpets prepared themselves to sound. 7 **The first (trumpet) sounded**, and there followed hail and fire, mixed with blood, and they were thrown to the earth. One third of the earth was burned up, and one third of the trees were burned up, and all green grass was burned up. 8 **The second angel sounded**, and something like a great burning mountain was thrown into the sea. One third of the sea became blood, 9 and one third of the living creatures which were in the sea died. One third of the ships were destroyed.*

> 10 **The third angel sounded**, and <u>a great star fell from the sky, burning like a torch</u>, and it fell on one third of the rivers, and on the springs of the waters. 11 The name of the star is called "Wormwood." One third of the waters became wormwood. Many people died from the waters, because they were made bitter* (poisonous).

> WEB Rev 8:12 ***The fourth angel sounded**, and one third of the sun was struck, and one third of the moon, and one third of the stars; so that one third of them would be darkened, and the day wouldn't shine for one third of it, and the night in the same way. 13 I saw, and I heard an eagle, flying in mid heaven, saying with a loud voice, <u>"Woe! Woe! Woe for those who dwell on the earth, because of the other voices of the trumpets of the three angels, who are yet to sound!"</u>*

> WEB Rev 9:1 ***The fifth angel sounded**, and I saw a star from the sky* (outer-space) *which had fallen to the earth. The key to the pit of the abyss was given to him. 2 He opened the pit of the abyss, and smoke went up out of the pit, like the smoke from a burning furnace. The sun and the air* (the sky) *were darkened because of the smoke from the pit. 3 Then out of the smoke came locusts on the earth, and power was given to them, as the scorpions of the earth have power. 4 They were told that they should not hurt the grass of the earth, neither any green thing, neither any tree, <u>but only those people who don't have God's seal on their foreheads</u>. 5 They were given power not to kill them, but to torment them for five months. Their torment was like the torment of a scorpion, when it strikes a person. 6 In those days people will seek death, and will in no way find it. They will desire to die, and death will flee from them. 7 The shapes of the locusts were like horses prepared for war. On their heads were something like golden crowns, and their faces were like people's faces. 8 They had hair like women's hair, and their teeth were like those of lions. 9 They had breastplates, like breastplates of iron. The sound of their wings was like the sound of chariots, or of many horses rushing to war. 10 They have tails like those of scorpions, and stings. In their tails they have power to harm men for five months. 11 They have over them as king the angel of the abyss. His name in Hebrew is "Abaddon", but in Greek, he has the name "Apollyon".*

Just as with the first four seals, these five trumpets are released simultaneously. The very thing that brings an end to the great tribulation is that heaven is silent no more, and intervenes by the release of these first five trumpets. There are three woes which are a part of the punishment of the global government and its people for the next 3-1/2 years. The three woes come one at a time with the release of the fifth, sixth, and seventh trumpets.

First, there are changes which happen to the very nature of the earth which are extremely punishing by themselves, making earth a hellish place to live for those who dwell on it. These come about from the first four trumpet blasts. Then, there are three woes. These woes are supernatural beings sent to punish, torment, kill, and destroy the kingdom of beast. The three woes are released one at a time and remain in the earth until Jesus crushes the eighth kingdom of the beast and ushers in His Kingdom from heaven. That means from beginning to end, by one type or another the earth will suffer from these woes for the last 3-1/2 years of the kingdom of the beast. In order to ensure that the three woes successively span the entire 3-1/2 years, the first woe (the fifth trumpet blast) must happen at the same time as the first trumpet blast. It is after that, that there is time between each woe or the remaining trumpet blasts. Here is a list of the woes:

1.   **The first woe:** released with the fifth trumpet blast is when the Devil and his angels are defeated in heaven and thrown out and down to the earth. Again, the fifth trumpet blast happens simultaneously with the four before it. The Devil and his angels become manifest as the earth enters into the spiritual realm from the physical universe at the same time. Then, as a part of the world's punishment, the Devil is allowed to release out of the Abyss scorpion like creatures which when stung, the sores they create give unbearable pain lasting for 5 months with each sting. They are not allowed to sting the elect with the mark of God on them.

2.   **The second woe:** released with the sixth trumpet blast is the release of an army of supernatural beings numbering 200,000,000. They circle the globe killing 1/3 of all humanity, except for those who have the mark of God on them. This is just in keeping with what the world did during the great tribulation. They killed 1/3 of the saints in that 3-1/2 year time period.

3.   **The third woe:** released with the seventh trumpet blast is the final showdown when seducing demons come out of the beast (antichrist), the false prophet (the beast out of the earth), and the Devil who is manifest to the people on the earth and they can see his form. They rally the people of the world to form an army in order to meet the Lord on the field of battle at Armageddon. This battle results in the "great supper of God." Every kind of scavenger bird there is, gorges themselves on the dead who thought they

could defeat the Lord in battle. Jesus then becomes the ruler of the entire globe and ushers in His 1,000 year Kingdom of Heaven, ruling from the New Jerusalem, which becomes the source of light for the whole world.

What happens at the seven trumpet blasts are described again in Revelation as a part of the second narrative. Only in that occasion they are referred to as the "seven bowls of God's wrath on the earth." This makes perfect sense. As each trumpet sounds its blast, the angel with its corresponding bowl of wrath pours it out on the earth. As is typical of Revelation and Biblical prophecy as the same subject is mention additional times, with each additional time new and different information is revealed about the subject. As a matter of fact, the subject is most often called something different than the previous.

In addition, the difference between the descriptions of the trumpet blasts and their corresponding bowls are structured similarly as the interludes. In that the trumpet blasts are the first part of an event and the description of the corresponding bowl is the resulting end of that same event. This helps encrypt the information about the subject as well as gives more details that when put together, provide a much more clearer and broader picture of the subject. This concept is supported in Daniel when it says:

Amp Da 12:3 And the teachers and those who are wise shall shine like the brightness of the firmament, and those who turn many to righteousness (to uprightness and right standing with God) [shall give forth light] like the stars forever and ever.
Amp Da 12:4 But you, O Daniel, shut up the words and seal the Book until the time of the end. [Then] many shall run to and fro and search anxiously [through the Book], and knowledge [of God's purposes as revealed by His prophets] shall be increased and become great.

Daniel's words were published, but they are sealed up and understanding is not released until the end. This is accomplished by how the whole story is spread out throughout the Bible and one has to search to and fro in the book to get all the details. It is sealed by it being encrypted through changing the description of the subject on each occasion mentioned making it difficult at best to associate one occasion with the next which tells about the same subject. Here is an example:

We read in the second narrative Rev 13:11-18 about an individual called a second or "another beast coming out of the earth." Then later on, in the same narrative, in verse 16:13 this same individual is referred to as the "false prophet." In the third narrative in verses 19:20, and 20:10 he again is referred to as the false prophet and no longer the beast coming out of the earth. Then in Daniel 9:26-27 he is referred to as the "other prince who will come . . ."

Amp Da 9:26 And after the sixty-two weeks [of years] shall the Anointed One be cut off or killed and shall have nothing [and no one] belonging to [and defending] Him. And the people of the [other] prince who will come will destroy the city and the sanctuary. Its end shall come with a flood; and even to the end there shall be war, and desolations are decreed.

Amp Da 9:27 And he shall enter into a strong and firm covenant with the many for one week [seven years]. And in the midst of the week he shall cause the sacrifice and offering to cease [for the remaining three and one-half years]; and upon the wing or pinnacle of abominations [shall come] one who makes desolate, until the full determined end is poured out on the desolator.

What these three references tell us is volumes. First of all, like the first beast he too is someone who had died and came back to life. We know this because he is called the second beast who came out of the earth, the grave. The first being Nimrod. Not first in order, but in importance. How do we verify this is the case? Although the Devil, in Revelation 19:20, is thrown into the Abyss after the defeat of the kingdom of the beast is crushed, the first and second beast are thrown alive into the lake of fire. This is in keeping with what it says about the first beast, when it says, he was, is now not, but will come up out of the Abyss on his way to his destruction.

Nimrod, the first beast, died thousands of years ago and because of his evil, was confined to the Abyss. However, he will rise from the dead, then suffer a second death by being thrown alive into the lake of fire (his destruction). No one goes into the lake of fire without having died once before, then was raised from death given a second body to be killed with. The lake of fire is the second death a soul must endure. Since it tells us that the second beast is thrown into the lake of fire with the first beast, this verifies that it is true that the second beast is someone who, likewise, had died and came back to life.

Next, he is called a false prophet. It is only by what he is described to do that we can tell the false prophet and the second beast is the same person. Knowing this, however, tells us that he is a spiritual type person of distinction that he is called a (false) prophet. Finally, he is called in Daniel the prince of the people to come who will destroy Jerusalem. That would make him sit in the seat of the emperor of Rome, the sixth kingdom of the beast. Then, it follows concerning the very same person (prince) that he stops the sacrifices in the temple at the midpoint of the last seven, and makes treaties with many along the way. This makes him the prince or king of the seventh kingdom because it is the same seat of power (Rome) as the sixth was.

According to the dream in Daniel the kingdom of iron legs mixes with the kingdom of clay feet. Unlike the other kingdoms, they merge instead of the previous being conquered by the next kingdom in line. That merging of the iron and the clay was the transition from the sixth kingdom to the seventh, from the Roman Empire to the Roman Church. That tells us that the prince who stops the sacrifices, and sets up the image bringing the first beast back to life is a pope of the Catholic Church.

NIV Rev 13:15 *He* (the beast out of the earth) *was given power to give breath to the image of the first beast . . .*

Revelation 13:15 makes the prince in Daniel who sets up the image or abomination in the temple, the same person as the beast out of the earth. So now what do we know about him through these three seemingly different individuals? The false prophet who creates an image of the beast, the antichrist, and brings it to life, is a pope of the Catholic Church—the leader of the seventh kingdom of the beast. A pope who will have had a death experience only to miraculously come back to life. In addition, he is a false prophet leading the Church away from God.

As Daniel stated, in order to understand one has to go to and fro, or back and forth in the pages of the Bible in order to piece everything together and therefore understand. That is because that is the way God designed the Bible and the way it remains encrypted needing His Spirit to reveal its true understanding. It is the same way with the trumpets and the bowls. They seem to tell different information and their orders do not line up. However, there is not a "fourteenness" to God's wrath, but a sevenness. An angel sounds a trumpet, and an angel pours out the corresponding bowl.

Therefore, as this is the case, in order to understand what goes on in those days, we must put them together looking at what they add up to. We must look at the sixth seal, and the seven bowls at the same time in order to fully understand the seven trumpets and the timing of their release. In that spirit we made two charts (below). One that outlines how they compare with each other and what that comparison tells us about their timing, and the other which parallels the seven trumpets next to the corresponding bowl.

The lines between the seven trumpets and the seven bowls are made to connect which trumpet is the same bowl giving additional information about each other.

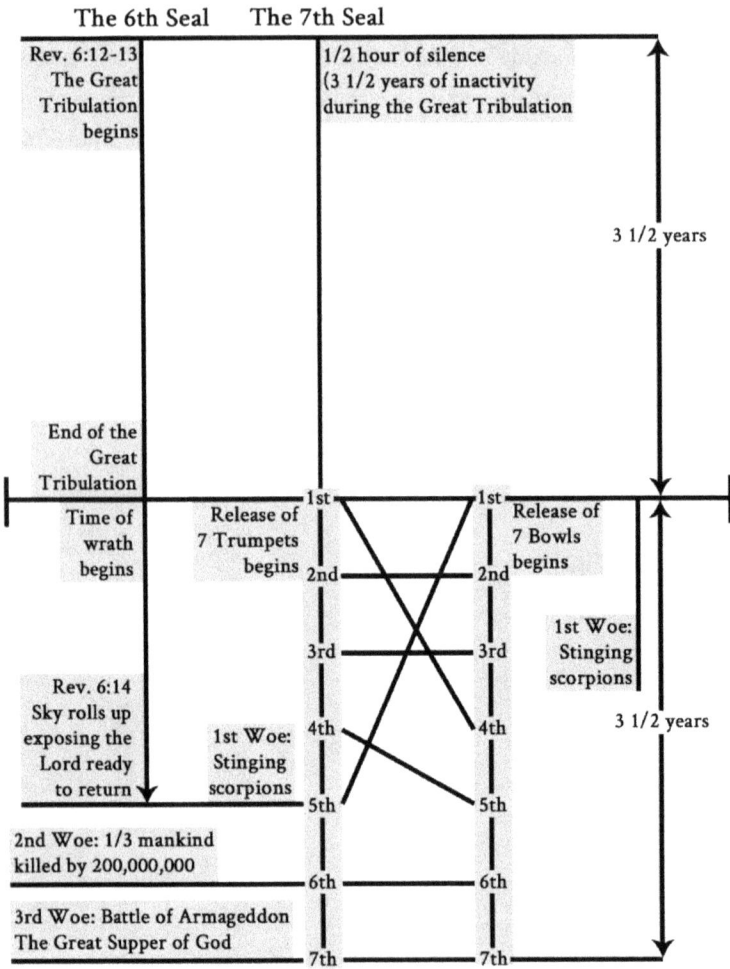

The 6th Seal   The 7th Seal

Rev. 6:12-13
The Great
Tribulation
begins

1/2 hour of silence
(3 1/2 years of inactivity
during the Great Tribulation

3 1/2 years

End of the
Great
Tribulation

Time of
wrath
begins

Release of
7 Trumpets
begins

1st   1st Release of
    7 Bowls
2nd 2nd begins

Rev. 6:14
Sky rolls up
exposing the
Lord ready
to return

1st Woe:
Stinging
scorpions

3rd 3rd

4th 4th

5th 5th

1st Woe:
Stinging
scorpions

3 1/2 years

2nd Woe: 1/3 mankind
killed by 200,000,000

6th 6th

3rd Woe: Battle of Armageddon
The Great Supper of God

7th 7th

The way this parallel chart works is that the trumpets on the left are paralleled on the right with its corresponding bowl of wrath, and not paralleled with the bowl in the same numeric order. This way we can add up together the meaning of each event, thereby gaining a fuller description of each event by putting them together, instead of comparing them.

Seven Trumpets and Seven Bowls Parallel Chart

The Seven Trumpets	The Seven Bowls of God's Wrath
WEB Rev 8:7 **The first sounded**, and there followed hail and fire, mixed with blood, and they were thrown to the earth. One third of the earth was burned up, and one third of the trees were burned up, and all green grass was burned up.	WEB Rev 16:8 **The fourth poured out his bowl** on the sun, and it was given to him to scorch men with fire. ⁹ People were scorched with great heat, and people blasphemed the name of God who has the power over these plagues. They didn't repent and give him glory.
WEB Rev 8:8 **The second angel sounded**, and something like a great burning mountain was thrown into the sea. One third of the sea became blood, ⁹ and one third of the living creatures which were in the sea died. One third of the ships were destroyed.	WEB Rev 16:3 **The second angel poured out his bowl** into the sea, and it became blood as of a dead man. Every living thing in the sea died.
WEB Rev 8:10 **The third angel sounded**, and a great star fell from the sky, burning	WEB Rev 16:4 **The third poured out his bowl** into the rivers and springs of

like a torch, and it fell on one third of the rivers, and on the springs of the waters. [11] The name of the star is called "Wormwood." One third of the waters became wormwood. Many people died from the waters, because they were made bitter.

water, and they became blood. [5] I heard the angel of the waters saying, "You are righteous, who are and who were, you Holy One, because you have judged these things. [6] For they poured out the blood of the saints and prophets, and you have given them blood to drink. They deserve this." [7] I heard the altar saying, "Yes, Lord God, the Almighty, true and righteous are your judgments."

WEB Rev 8:12 **The fourth angel sounded,** and one third of the sun was struck, and one third of the moon, and one third of the stars; so that one third of them would be darkened, and the day wouldn't shine for one third of it, and the night in the same way. [13] I saw, and I heard an eagle, flying in mid heaven, saying with a loud voice, "Woe! Woe! Woe for those who dwell on the earth, because of the other voices of the trumpets of the three angels, who are yet to sound!"

WEB Rev 16:10 **The fifth poured out his bowl** on the throne of the beast, and his kingdom was darkened. They gnawed their tongues because of the pain, [11] and they blasphemed the God of heaven because of their pains and their sores. They didn't repent of their works

WEB Rev 9:1 **The fifth angel sounded,** and I saw a star from the sky which had fallen to the earth. The key to the pit of the abyss was given to him. [2] He opened the pit of the abyss, and smoke went up out of the pit, like the smoke from a burning furnace. The sun and the air were darkened because of the smoke from the pit. [3] Then out of the smoke

WEB Rev 16:2 **The first went, and poured out his bowl** into the earth, and it became a harmful and evil sore on the people who had the mark of the beast, and who worshiped his image.

came locusts on the earth, and power was given to them, as the scorpions of the earth have power. ⁴ They were told that they should not hurt the grass of the earth, neither any green thing, neither any tree, but only those people who don't have God's seal on their foreheads. ⁵ They were given power not to kill them, but to torment them for five months. Their torment was like the torment of a scorpion, when it strikes a person. ⁶ In those days people will seek death, and will in no way find it. They will desire to die, and death will flee from them. ⁷ The shapes of the locusts were like horses prepared for war. On their heads were something like golden crowns, and their faces were like people's faces. ⁸ They had hair like women's hair, and their teeth were like those of lions. ⁹ They had breastplates, like breastplates of iron. The sound of their wings was like the sound of chariots, or of many horses rushing to war. ¹⁰ They have tails like those of scorpions, and stings. In their tails they have power to harm men for five months. ¹¹ They have over them as king the angel of the abyss. His name in Hebrew is "Abaddon", but in Greek, he has the name "Apollyon". ¹² The first woe is past. Behold, there are still two woes coming after this.

WEB Rev 9:13 **The sixth angel sounded.** I

WEB Rev 16:12 **The sixth poured out his**

heard a voice from the horns of the golden altar which is before God, [14] saying to the sixth angel who had the trumpet, "Free the four angels who are bound at the great river Euphrates!" [15] The four angels were freed who had been prepared for that hour and day and month and year, so that they might kill one third of mankind. [16] The number of the armies of the horsemen was two hundred million. I heard the number of them. [17] Thus I saw the horses in the vision, and those who sat on them, having breastplates of fiery red, hyacinth blue, and sulfur yellow; and the horses' heads resembled lions' heads. Out of their mouths proceed fire, smoke, and sulfur. [18] By these three plagues were one third of mankind killed: by the fire, the smoke, and the sulfur, which proceeded out of their mouths. [19] For the power of the horses is in their mouths, and in their tails. For their tails are like serpents, and have heads, and with them they harm. [20] The rest of mankind, who were not killed with these plagues, didn't repent of the works of their hands, that they wouldn't worship demons, and the idols of gold, and of silver, and of brass, and of stone, and of wood; which can't see, hear, or walk. [21] They didn't repent of their murders, their sorceries, their sexual immorality, or their thefts.

bowl on the great river, the Euphrates. Its water was dried up, that the way might be prepared for the kings that come from the sunrise. [13] I saw coming out of the mouth of the dragon, and out of the mouth of the beast, and out of the mouth of the false prophet, three unclean spirits, something like frogs; [14] for they are spirits of demons, performing signs; which go out to the kings of the whole inhabited earth, to gather them together for the war of that great day of God, the Almighty. [15] "Behold, I come like a thief. Blessed is he who watches, and keeps his clothes, so that he doesn't walk naked, and they see his shame." [16] He gathered them together into the place which is called in Hebrew, Megiddo *(Armageddon)*.

WEB Rev 11:15 **The seventh angel sounded**, and great voices in heaven followed, saying, "The kingdom of the world has become the Kingdom of our Lord, and of his Christ. He will reign forever and ever!" [16] The twenty-four elders, who sit on their thrones before God's throne, fell on their faces and worshiped God, [17] saying: "We give you thanks, Lord God, the Almighty, the one who is and who was; because you have taken your great power, and reigned. [18] The nations were angry, and your wrath came, as did the time for the dead to be judged, and to give your bondservants the prophets, their reward, as well as to the saints, and those who fear your name, to the small and the great; and to destroy those who destroy the earth." [19] God's temple that is in heaven was opened, and the ark of the Lord's covenant was seen in his temple. Lightnings, sounds, thunders, an earthquake, and great hail followed.

WEB Rev 16:17 **The seventh poured out his bowl** into the air. A loud voice came out of the temple of heaven, from the throne, saying, "It is done!" [18] There were lightnings, sounds, and thunders; and there was a great earthquake, such as was not since there were men on the earth, so great an earthquake, so mighty. [19] The great city was divided into three parts, and the cities of the nations fell. Babylon the great was remembered in the sight of God, to give to her the cup of the wine of the fierceness of his wrath. [20] Every island fled away, and the mountains were not found. [21] Great hailstones, about the weight of a talent, came down out of the sky on people. People blasphemed God because of the plague of the hail, for this plague is exceedingly severe.

What we have to consider to unpack the vision is that the trumpet blast and the bowls are a description of the same event. We know this because the number seven is used. That means what the trumpets and bowls describe is the sevenness of God's wrath on the world. They have to be further descriptions of the same sevenness of His wrath, otherwise the *structure of sevens* used in the book of Revelation is inconsistent or violated. Therefore, if the first thing that happens with the trumpets happens at the same time as the first thing with the bowls, then every bowl and trumpet between the two will happen at the same time, even if they are not in corresponding numeric order.

Here is the first thing to observe. That on the left or trumpet side it typically states a third of this or that happens. Then on the right or bowl side when talking about the same event it typically reads that all or everything is affected when the same thing happens. What this means is one side describes the initial and the other the eventual. Or, one describes the beginning of an event and the other describes the resulting end.

Let's take an example: When the fourth trumpet sounds, the earth crowns into the spiritual realm. This results in the sky, from horizon to horizon, during its 24 hour cycle is an 8 hour view of the day sky (the sun), an 8 hour view of the night sky (the stars and the moon), and an 8 hour view of the spiritual realm—a third, third and third. If not for the sight of the Lord ready to come down to the earth (the sign of the coming of the Son of Man), when the view of the sky is facing the spirit realm there would be total darkness because there are no heavenly bodies to be a source of light; like there are in the natural universe. This would be the initial or beginning of the event. However, when the corresponding bowl is poured out it states that the kingdom of the beast is plunged into total darkness. Total darkness is the eventual or resulting end of the same event that begins with a third of darkness.

This makes it easier to understand when Jesus talks about the same event. He does not describe it in part or in stages, but in full—the eventual results of the event. Let us look and see:

NIV Mt 24:23 At that time if anyone says to you, 'Look, here is the Christ!' or, 'There he is!' do not believe it.

NIV Mt 24:24 For false Christs and false prophets will appear and perform great signs and miracles to deceive even the elect—if that were possible.

NIV Mt 24:25 See, I have told you ahead of time.

NIV Mt 24:26 "So if anyone tells you, 'There he is, out in the desert,' do not go out; or, 'Here he is, in the inner rooms,' do not believe it.

NIV Mt 24:27 For as lightning that comes from the east is visible even in the west, so will be the coming of the Son of Man.

NIV Mt 24:28 Wherever there is a carcass, there the vultures will gather.

NIV Mt 24:29 *"Immediately after the distress of those days*

". . . the distress of those days" is referring to the 3-1/2 years of the great tribulation. This statement, "Immediately after" agrees with the book of Revelation when it reveals that it is the events of the first 5 trumpets that actually put an end to the great tribulation.

" 'the sun will be darkened, and the moon will not give its light; the stars will fall from the sky, and the heavenly bodies will be shaken.'
NIV Mt 24:30 *"At that time the sign of the Son of Man will appear in the sky, and all the nations of the earth will mourn. They will see the Son of Man coming on the clouds of the sky, with power and great glory.*

Jesus, is now describing the first four trumpets and bowls by what He stated above. It is the tearing of the fabric of space and time, and the earth being delivered into the spiritual realm bringing eventual total darkness over the whole earth. These circumstances facilitate the sign of the coming of the Son of Man. That sign is Jesus visible in the sky, horizon to horizon, poised to come back to earth and administer justice.

NIV Mt 24:31 *And he will send his angels with a loud trumpet call, and they will gather his elect from the four winds, from one end of the heavens to the other.*

What Jesus is describing is the "first resurrection" and the second rapture. This is when both, those who have died in the great tribulation and those who survived it without coming off their testimony, having not worshiped the beast or taken his mark, receive their celestial bodies. Then, together, are caught up to the sky to take their place behind Jesus before He descends back to earth.

Jesus does not explain the two different phases of this event but simply the end result of the same event.

By these three factors combined together:

- the seven trumpets and the corresponding seven bowls listed in the order they are

- what is included within the sixth seal
- the first woe being released at the beginning of His wrath

This information tells us, in God's cryptic way, the order and timing of these events giving us a clue as to what is released the moment the great tribulation ends, and the wrath of God against the world begins:

NIV Rev 6:12 I watched as he opened the sixth seal. There was a great earthquake. The sun turned black like sackcloth made of goat hair, the whole moon turned blood red,
NIV Rev 6:13 and the stars in the sky fell to earth, as late figs drop from a fig tree when shaken by a strong wind.
NIV Rev 6:14 The sky receded like a scroll, rolling up, and every mountain and island was removed from its place.
NIV Rev 6:15 Then the kings of the earth, the princes, the generals, the rich, the mighty, and every slave and every free man hid in caves and among the rocks of the mountains.
NIV Rev 6:16 They called to the mountains and the rocks, "Fall on us and hide us from the face of him who sits on the throne and from the wrath of the Lamb!
NIV Rev 6:17 For the great day of their wrath has come, and who can stand?"

The stars falling to earth like late figs from a tree in a strong wind is the killing of the Christians during the time of the great tribulation. Verses 12 and 13 (above) starts with the earthquake which occurs when the two witnesses and the *Church Pure* are caught up to heaven as a part of the Holy Spirit withdrawing from the earth. This also is fulfillment of and makes true what Jesus promised after the Last Supper.

NIV Jn 14:15 "If you love me, you will obey what I command.
NIV Jn 14:16 And I will ask the Father, and he will give you another Counselor to be with you forever—
NIV Jn 14:17 the Spirit of truth. The world cannot accept him, because it neither sees him nor knows him. But you know him, for he lives with you and will be in you.
NIV Jn 14:18 I will not leave you as orphans; I will come to you.
NIV Jn 14:19 Before long, the world will not see me anymore, but you will see me. Because I live, you also will live.
NIV Jn 14:20 On that day you will realize that I am in my Father, and you are in me, and I am in you.

"Before long the world will not see me any longer. . ." is not referring to His death on the cross because He remains in the world by His Spirit and through the bodies of those in union with Him. Rather it is referring to later when he finally departs this world completely, both in Spirit and body, even His body, the Church. That is when the desolation comes, His Spirit withdraws from the earth, and His body (the *Church Pure*) is raptured.

He just got finished saying that He would not leave us as orphans and that He will be with us forever. Given He is leaving and the world will not see Him anymore and as a result of His promise to be in us forever, the next thing He says is "On that day you will realize that I am in my Father, and you are in me, and I am in you." What day is He talking about? When He finally leaves the earth, Spirit and body, the day of the rapture, the day of the desolation caused by the abomination of the beast coming back to life as a manmade Frankenstein! We will realize it because we will be raptured before His heavenly throne clothed in our celestial bodies and having made that transition without so much as tasting death. We will continue to see Him when the world will no more because He is not there. However, we are instead present with Him where he goes—we are not there for the world to see us either.

"The sun turned black like sackcloth made of goat hair, the whole moon turned blood red, and the stars in the sky fell to earth, as late figs drop from a fig tree when shaken by a strong wind." Is all representative of the spiritual darkness which overtakes the earth when the Spirit and the bride (the *Church Pure*) departs with the two witness. The blood red moon and the stars falling are representative of the great tribulation and the genocide of the Christians who remain—the *Church Corrupt*.

Then verses 14 through 17 (below) are referencing the beginning of the wrath of God 3-1/2 years later. Its description brings us all the way to the fifth trumpet and first bowl. Making reference to the sky rolling up and the sign in the sky of the Son of Man poised to return. This is part of the first woe, the fifth trumpet.

NIV Rev 6:14 *The sky receded like a scroll, rolling up, and every mountain and island was removed from its place.*
NIV Rev 6:15 *Then the kings of the earth, the princes, the generals, the rich, the mighty, and every slave and every free man hid in caves and among the rocks of the mountains.*

NIV Rev 6:16 *They called to the mountains and the rocks, "Fall on us and hide us from the face of him who sits on the throne and from the wrath of the Lamb!*
NIV Rev 6:17 *For the great day of their wrath has come, and who can stand?"*

These verses even make reference to the stinging scorpions of the first woe when they called on the rock to fall on them and kill them. We had been told that their sting is so painful that people will seek death and not find it.

It is important to note that this is as far as the vision goes when talking about the bride, or Church being present during the sounding of the trumpets.

Again, all this added together tells us that the first five trumpets and bowls happen simultaneously, all of which brings an abrupt end to the great tribulation.

We can also understand that the first four trumpets and bowls are what you might call natural disasters, or even as the insurance companies would call them, "acts of God." Then the three succeeding woes are calamities perpetrated by spiritual beings. The last being Jesus Himself defeating the world government to rule it as His own Kingdom. It aids in interpreting, recognizing that the first four trumpets as natural disasters and the last three as supernatural beings who bring harm to humans. It helps in that we can, for example, know when to interpret stars as physical objects and when as living beings. As a note, the first 3-1/2 years of wrath against the *Church Corrupt* was carried out by human agents.

Let us take a look at the first four trumpets, and bowls of natural disasters they visit upon the earth, including the first woe—the fifth trumpet.

The day that the full number of the combined groups of the 144,000 and the great multitude have reached their fullness, the half an hour of silence or inactivity ceases. Not another single person who would be the bride and celestial humans who rule the earth with Jesus for 1,000 years will be killed ever again! The close of the great tribulation has come 3-1/2 years after the day the Holy Spirit, the two witnesses, and the *Church Pure* left the earth. The beast has had his 42 months of unrestrained domination of the globe.

One of the primary requirements for the end to happen is that the accuser of the brethren, the Devil, must become prohibited from standing before God on His throne, presenting and justifying to God why His elect deserve death—the prosecutor. This must be accomplished for each life even though they may be one of God's people. Since the garden, God has kept His love and compassion in check by letting the Devil rail against humans as a type of prosecutor, being a constant reminder of their sin so that He, the Lord, would be just in all His verdicts.

However, the Devil has performed this duty with corrupt motives, to first, cause people to sin against God dividing from Him. Then, to have God separate from them because of their unfaithfulness. Although the Devil has had ulterior motives in carrying out his duty and evil passion, God has never been fooled or seduced into serving either the agenda of the Devil or injustice. Rather, this tolerance of allowing the Devil to constantly rail against His people, has kept God and His justice righteous and impartial.

This event of Michael arresting and expelling the Devil and his followers (angels) from the heavenly court of God is described as a part of the first woe and fifth trumpet:

NRSV Rev 9:1 And the fifth angel blew his trumpet, and I saw a star that had fallen from heaven to earth, and he (note that the star is called a "he" as in a person and not a celestial body) *was given the key to the shaft of the bottomless pit;*

That star is Satan, the Devil, a celestial being whose natural habitat is in heaven. He has literally been cast out of heaven (the court of God) down to the earth where he becomes manifest to the people of the earth. From this point forward, he no longer has access to God and no longer will he slander the saints of God in His presence. His mouth has been silenced in the court of God, never to have that place again! He is called a star in this passage just as were the saints of the sixth seal who held heavenly stature by the Holy Spirit of God in them. He tossed them down to the earth—the grave—meaning he killed their mortal body, however, they did not lose their heavenly stature.

Although their body died and was buried in the earth (cast down), the Spirit and soul within the saints whose stature was heavenly did not lose their heavenly stature. Their spirit was merely prevented from reaching down to the earth where their feet walked on. They instead are later raised from the dead, receive a celestial body and their new habitat becomes the spiritual realm. Their new stature is before the throne of God in His court. The irony here is that the Devil who cast down those stars to the earth by killing the saints during the great tribulation, is now himself cast down. However, unlike the saints, he loses his heavenly stature as a star. Instead of experiencing an ascension, he has experienced a dissent both to the earth, and in stature. Soon he will fall further when he is cast down into the bottomless pit.

NRSV Rev 9:2 he opened the shaft of the bottomless pit, and from the shaft rose smoke like the smoke of a great furnace, and the sun and the air were darkened with the smoke from the shaft. 3 Then from the smoke came locusts on the earth, and they were given authority like the authority of scorpions of the earth.

The Devil opens the Abyss/the bottomless pit and lets loose the other part of the first woe—the scorpion type creatures.

NRSV Rev 9:4 They were told not to damage the grass of the earth or any green growth or any tree, but only those people who do not have the seal of God on their foreheads. 5 They were allowed to torture them for five months, but not to kill them, and their torture was like the torture of a scorpion when it stings someone. 6 And in those days people will seek death but will not find it; they will long to die, but death will flee from them.

NRSV Rev 9:7 In appearance the locusts were like horses equipped for battle. On their heads were what looked like crowns of gold; their faces were like human faces, 8 their hair like women's hair, and their teeth like lions' teeth; 9 they had scales like iron breastplates, and the noise of their wings was like the noise of many chariots with horses rushing into battle. 10 They have tails like scorpions, with stingers, and in their tails is their power to harm people for five months. 11 They have as king over them the angel of the bottomless pit; his name in Hebrew is Abaddon, and in Greek he is called Apollyon.

This same exact event is described again in the second narrative, Rev 12:3-17:

NRSV Rev 12:3 Then another portent (sign) *appeared in heaven: a great red dragon, with seven heads and ten horns, and seven diadems on his heads. ⁴ His tail swept down a third of the stars of heaven and threw them to the earth* (the killing of the saints during the great tribulation). *Then the dragon stood before the woman who was about to bear a child, so that he might devour her child as soon as it was born. ⁵ And she gave birth to a son, a male child, who is to rule all the nations with a rod of iron. But her child was snatched away and taken to God and to his throne* (this is the rapture of the Church Pure, the body of Christ*); ⁶ and the woman (the Jews and Israelites) fled into the wilderness, where she has a place prepared by God, so that there she can be nourished for one thousand two hundred sixty days.*

NRSV Rev 12:7 And war broke out in heaven; Michael and his angels fought against the dragon. The dragon and his angels fought back, ⁸ but they were defeated, and there was no longer any place for them in heaven. ⁹ The great dragon was thrown down, that ancient serpent, who is called the Devil and Satan, the deceiver of the whole world--he was thrown down to the earth, and his angels were thrown down with him.

This (above) is the end of the great tribulation and the beginning of the wrath of God poured out on the people of the kingdom of the beast. Here is some additional information we are told about this event which is the fifth trumpet. It is when the Devil is cast down including the angels who are in league with him and his evil.

NRSV Rev 12:10 Then I heard a loud voice in heaven, proclaiming, "Now have come the salvation and the power and the kingdom of our God and the authority of his Messiah, for the accuser of our comrades has been thrown down, who accuses them day and night before our God.

Satan, A.K.A. the "star," falls from heaven to the earth.

NRSV Rev 12:11 But they have conquered him by the blood of the Lamb and by the word of their testimony, for they did not cling to life even in the face of death.
¹² Rejoice then, you heavens and those who dwell in them! But woe to the earth and the sea for the devil has come down to you with great wrath, because he knows that his time is short!" So when the dragon saw that he had been thrown down to the earth, he pursued ⁴⁰ the woman who had given birth to the male child. ¹⁴ But the woman was given the two wings of the great

eagle, so that she could fly from the serpent into the wilderness, to her place where she is
nourished for a time, and times, and half a time.

Once again the Israelites are given a place to hide in the desert during this time of wrath. Previously, they were given a place to hide during the great tribulation.

Note: When it comes to the Christians, the *Church Pure* was raptured becoming celestial humans before the great tribulation. As far as the *Church Corrupt* if they died during the great tribulation (given their faithfulness) they are included in the first resurrection. Then along with those faithful who survive the great tribulation they and the resurrected will be raptured to meet, the now visible, Jesus in the sky also becoming celestial humans.

Those who survive the great tribulation are given a mark of God so that none of the three woes or their enemies in the world can harm them. That covers the Christians. On both occasions the Israelites are given a place to be safe from all 7 years of wrath from God. Why? As a part of His 1,000 year reign, Jesus is going to restore Israel. As such, they must not be genocide like the Christians or there will not be many left to populate Israel when Jesus comes into His Kingdom. Likewise, if Jesus made them celestial humans they would reside in the New Jerusalem as a spiritual being and again leaving few mortal humans for Jesus to populate Israel with.

The Israelites were meant to be the bride, the celestial humans who ruled the mortal humans on the earth during the Lord's 1,000 year reign. However, they forfeited that place as His bride, and that place was therefore passed onto the Christians. Those who were to be the first, now are the last to become celestial humans and those meant to be last, the gentile, became first. The Israelites will have to wait until the last day and be judged, then be found worthy to become celestial humans and a part of the new earth and new heavens.

In the backdrop of the first woe, the supernatural invading the natural can happen because the natural earth and its atmosphere moves into the spiritual realm, where there is no solar system, no stars, suns or planets, even galaxies. There is nothing but darkness. That is with the exception of an 8 hour view from horizon to horizon of the Lord ready to come back to earth and bring justice with Him. The people of the earth rich and poor, strong and weak all want the mountains to fall on them seeking death, for a few reasons. The first being the sign of the coming of Jesus in the sky, just as He had predicted. The second, which is inferred, the agonizing and relentless pain of the sting of these supernatural creatures, which when described says men will seek death because of their agony but it will elude them. The third is all the upheaval, the crinkling, warping and shaking of the earth and the heavenly bodies (including the sun) caused by the dimensional shift of the earth upsetting the very fabric of space and time. All of which cause the people to believe the end of the world is at hand.

The first four trumpets and bowls describe well the effect this has on planet earth. The way these violent and devastating events happen are so encompassing that they initially affect a third, we are told. However, they set in motion their devastation until the entire globe is impacted. For example, we go from only a third of the view of the sky facing the spirit realm, to the entire earth being born into the spirit realm where there is no light whatsoever illuminating the earth.

Jesus told us that when this happens the heavenly bodies are shaken as well. This may cause the sun to flare. In addition, because of the fabric of space and time crinkling like an accordion in order to create an opening so the earth can pass through, the distance between the earth and the sun is shortened. This causes the sun to scorch the earth with its rays. Even still perhaps the ozone layer is damaged or destroyed in this process. Nevertheless, the grass and the trees burn up in the heat as well as many buildings and homes.

So violent is this movement that the mountains topple and the islands are washed away. The earth quakes so bad that all the cities are leveled and their infrastructure destroyed. Highways and bridges destroyed. Life as we know it comes to a halt. Fresh water, sanitation, energy, and provisions are all interrupted, and become scarce.

NIV Rev 14:19 The angel swung his sickle on the earth, gathered its grapes and threw them into the great winepress of God's wrath.
NIV Rev 14:20 They were trampled in the winepress outside the city, and blood flowed out of the press, rising as high as the horses' bridles for a distance of 1,600 stadia.

As a result of the great tribulation, the blood of the saints flows like a river 4 to 6 feet deep for over 200 miles. Given a person has about 5 quarts of blood, how many perish in the great tribulation which can spill enough blood to make up that quantity? Whatever the answer is, we are told:

WEB Rev 16:4 *The third poured out his bowl into the rivers and springs of water, and they became blood.* *5 I heard the angel of the waters saying, "You are righteous, who are and who were, you Holy One, because you have judged these things.* *6 For they poured out the blood of the saints and prophets, and you have given them blood to drink. They deserve this."* *7 I heard the altar saying, "Yes, Lord God, the Almighty, true and righteous are your judgments."*

Just as in Egypt, however, this plague from God once again affects not just one nation but a third of the earth in its initial devastation. Then progresses to effect the entire globe.

John tells us that a meteor like object the size of a mountain top comes down like a fireball, smashing into the oceans destroying life in them as well as creating tsunamis which destroy the ships that sail on them.

All this and the first woe falls upon the earth as a suddenly of God! On the earth, chaos, disorder, and every man for himself will rule. Try as they may, governments will not be able to keep order. The death toll because of all this devastation can only be exceeded by the next two woes.

WEB Rev 9:12 *The first woe is past. Behold, there are still two woes coming after this.*

WEB Rev 9:13 **The sixth angel sounded.** *I heard a voice from the horns of the golden altar which is before God,* *14 saying to the sixth angel who had the trumpet, "Free the four angels who are bound at the great river Euphrates!"*

WEB Rev 9:15 *The four angels were freed who had been prepared for that hour and day and month and year, so that they might kill one third of mankind.*

WEB Rev 9:16 *The number of the armies of the horsemen was two hundred million. I heard the number of them.* *17 Thus I saw the horses in the vision, and those who sat on them, having breastplates of fiery red, hyacinth blue, and sulfur yellow; and the horses' heads resembled lions' heads. Out of their mouths proceed fire, smoke, and sulfur.*

It is interesting to note that the colors of the city Babylon were blue and yellow. The mascot or symbol of Babylon is the lion. To this day the gates of Ishtar (Nimrod's wife) with its blue and yellow brick walls and statues of lions remain in a museum in Germany.

> *WEB Rev 9:18 By these three plagues were one third of mankind killed: by the fire, the smoke, and the sulfur, which proceeded out of their mouths. 19 For the power of the horses is in their mouths, and in their tails. For their tails are like serpents, and have heads, and with them they harm. 20 The rest of mankind, who were not killed with these plagues, didn't repent of the works of their hands, that they wouldn't worship demons, and the idols of gold, and of silver, and of brass, and of stone, and of wood; which can't see, hear, or walk. 21 They didn't repent of their (1) murders, (2) their sorceries, (3) their sexual immorality, or (4) their thefts.*

The second woe is the release of the army of 200,000,000 supernatural creatures from the Abyss who circle the globe and kill one third of mankind. This matches the amount of believers the world killed during the great tribulation.

The second interlude:

The angel and the little scroll

> *WEB Rev 10:1 I saw a mighty angel coming down out of the sky, clothed with a cloud. A rainbow was on his head. His face was like the sun, and his feet like pillars of fire. 2 He had in his hand a little open book (scroll). He set his right foot on the sea, and his left on the land. 3 He cried with a loud voice, as a lion roars. When he cried, the seven thunders uttered their voices.*

Here is the second interlude. The narrative comes to a temporary halt to interject a truth which will bring meaning to this narrative the Lord is revealing. The framework by which we need to understand and interpret this second interlude is the same as the first. That is to say, as a context about what is said we need to see the first part as the beginning of the same subject or event and the second part the end of the same event. Considering these verses in that framework actually aids us in this case in interpretation.

> *WEB Rev 10:4 When the seven thunders sounded, I was about to write; but I heard a voice from the sky saying, "Seal up the things which the seven thunders said, and don't write them." 5 The angel whom I saw standing on the sea and on the land lifted up his right hand to the sky, 6 and swore by him who lives forever and ever, who created heaven and the things that are in it, the earth and the things that are in it, and the sea and the things that are in it, that there will no longer be*

delay, [7] but in the days of the voice of the seventh angel, when he is about to sound, then the mystery of God is finished, as he declared to his servants, the prophets.

The use of the word "angel" is not referring to a certain class or species of heavenly creatures. Angel simply means: messenger. As such, the word can apply to a man or spirit being. This being most certainly is a messenger because of the scroll in his hand. This messenger is none other than Jesus, the Son of God. The message is the good news of the Gospel, the message which brings salvation to all who hear it and believe.

NAS REV 10:1 I saw another strong angel coming down out of heaven, clothed with a cloud; and the rainbow was upon his head, and his face was like the sun, and his feet like pillars of fire

The vision of Eve revealed her as clothed with the sun and had a crown of 12 stars upon her head. Those 12 stars were the purpose and destiny which God had crowned her with. They are the 12 tribes of Israel through who the Christ would be born from. Both the Devil and his beast/antichrist have 7 heads (kingdoms) with seven crowns (kings) having been granted that destiny as a part of judgment against the world. Jesus comes crowned with a rainbow. The purpose and destiny God had crowned Him with is the promise He made to Noah. That He would not destroy humanity in a flood again. A flood which only 8 humans survived. Although the world has been judged to be destroyed with fire bringing natural humans to total extinction, God sent His Christ to the world not as part of His judgment but as part of His salvation of man.

NAS JN 12:47 "If anyone hears My sayings and does not keep them, I do not judge him; for I did not come to judge the world, but to save the world.
NAS JN 12:48 " He who rejects Me and does not receive My sayings, has one who judges him; the word I spoke is what will judge him at the last day.

By the release of His Spirit everyone in union with Him becomes celestial humans. They survive the destruction of the natural world and all in it. They transcend the natural universe, become a different species of humans, able to live in a different dimensional realm; clothed with a body that is adapted and suited for that realm. He does not save 8 giving them a second chance, but "multitudes beyond counting" in keeping with the promise His Father made to Noah. His message on the scroll is indeed good news for those (us) who are perishing.

NIV Rev 10:2 And in his hand was a small scroll, which he had unrolled.

That scroll is the scroll John saw that was given to Jesus before the throne, of which He broke the seals to reveal its contents. It is now opened in this vision! It is the Revelation the Father gave to Jesus to give to His Church. The contents of that scroll is the message of the Gospel Jesus came to the earth to give those who would believe. Within it we find that in the midst of judgment being carried out which will destroy the earth and make natural humans extinct, there is a way to be saved by becoming a celestial human and escaping the fate of every natural human. That way is to believe, trust in and obey, while wholly conforming to the Revelation and message within that scroll as brought to us by Jesus, the only one worthy to receive this knowledge and give it to His Church. Why? Because He sacrificed His life for them to have the salvation offered and prescribed within that scroll which formerly had 7 seals keeping it hidden. Here, at this point of Revelation (during the second interlude), that scroll is finally opened with seals broken;

NIV Rev 10:2 And in his hand was a small scroll, <u>which he had unrolled.</u>

Only Jesus could carry out and bring us the plan God had that would bring an end to the earth and those upon it while somehow keeping His promise to Noah. This is why, along with the opened scroll which reveals that plan (the Gospel) Jesus has around His head a rainbow—the sign of that promise. Indeed, this is good news! For those who believe, God provided a way out from the doom that has already been loosed. No one listened to or believed the preaching of Noah, God's prophet, and joined him on the ark. However, multitudes beyond counting listened and believed Jesus and are saved.

NIV Rev 1:1 <u>The revelation of Jesus Christ, which God gave him to show his servants what must soon take place. He made it known by sending his angel to his servant John,</u>
NIV Rev 1:2 <u>who testifies to everything he saw—that is, the word of God and the testimony of Jesus Christ.</u>

NIV Rev 1:3 Blessed is the one who reads the words of this prophecy, and blessed are those who hear it and take to heart what is written in it, because the time is near.

"He cried with a loud voice, as a lion roars. When he cried, the seven thunders uttered their voices." This is Jesus, the Lion of the tribe of Judah spreading the good news of the Gospel—that which His Father gave to Jesus to give to us. When He spoke the sevenfold Spirit of God first of all witnessed in the hearts of His hearers that what He spoke is from God. In addition, that same sevenfold Spirit uttered His message through those who preached His words witnessing in the hearts of their hearers that their words are from God. In other words, the sevenfold Spirit remains in the earth and continues to resonate and witness as true in the heart of every hearer what Jesus spoke 2,000 years ago. Just as the day He spoke them the powerful conviction of His words 2,000 years later has not diminished whatsoever when one hears them for the first time.

When He swears there will be no more delay, He is talking about His sacrificial act on the cross. Why should He swear by the earth and the sea and the people and things in them? Isn't it enough that He swears by the Father of all creation? He is not under those He is swearing by that they would have a power over Him if He fails. He swears not only by His Father but by all that His death will serve! He swears to them that He will give Himself up as a sacrifice for their salvation from the judgment of fire that all in the earth would otherwise suffer.

> *WEB Rev 10:8 The voice which I heard from heaven, again speaking with me, said, "Go, take the book (scroll) which is open in the hand of the angel who stands on the sea and on the land." 9 I went to the angel, telling him to give me the little book (scroll). He said to me, "Take it, and eat it up. It will make your stomach bitter, but in your mouth it will be as sweet as honey." 10 I took the little book (scroll) out of the angel's hand, and ate it up. It was as sweet as honey in my mouth. When I had eaten it, my stomach was made bitter. 11 They told me, "You must prophesy again over many peoples, nations, languages, and kings."*

John eating of the scroll is him ingesting the message of the salvation of Jesus deep into his spirit. Perhaps it was the sweetness of the sacrificial love of the salvation from Jesus that made the message in the scroll like honey going down. However, ingesting and understanding, or getting it into his heart what it would demand of Jesus to make that sweet and free salvation possible, made him sour in his guts.

NIV Jn 14:27 *Peace I leave with you; my peace I give you. I do not give to you as the world gives.* *Do not let your hearts be troubled and do not be afraid.*

NIV Jn 14:28 *"You heard me say, 'I am going away and I am coming back to you.' If you loved me, you would be glad that I am going to the Father, for the Father is greater than I.*

NIV Jn 16:5 *"Now I am going to him who sent me, yet none of you asks me, 'Where are you going?'*

NIV Jn 16:6 *Because I have said these things, you are filled with grief.*

John is told to seal the words up and not write them down. Yet that he would later, "prophesy <u>again</u> over many peoples, nations, and kings." When Jesus was with them (John) His instructions were:

NIV Mt 10:5 *These twelve Jesus sent out with the following instructions: <u>"Do not go among the</u>* *<u>Gentiles or enter any town of the Samaritans.</u>*

NIV Mt 10:6 *<u>Go rather to the lost sheep of Israel.</u>*

NIV Mt 10:7 *As you go, preach this message: 'The kingdom of heaven is near.'*

NIV Mt 10:8 *Heal the sick, raise the dead, cleanse those who have leprosy, drive out demons.* *Freely you have received, freely give.*

Then after Jesus did what He swore to do, suffering the cross, He then changed His directive to:

NIV Mt 28:16 *Then the eleven disciples went to Galilee, to the mountain where Jesus had told them to go.*

NIV Mt 28:17 *When they saw him, they worshiped him; but some doubted.*

NIV Mt 28:18 *Then Jesus came to them and said, "All authority in heaven and on earth has been given to me.*

NIV Mt 28:19 *Therefore go and <u>make disciples of all nations,</u> baptizing them in the name of the Father and of the Son and of the Holy Spirit,*

NIV Mt 28:20 *and teaching them to obey everything I have commanded you. And surely I am with you always, to the very end of the age."*

The two witnesses

WEB Rev 11:1 A reed like a rod was given to me. Someone said, "Rise, and measure God's temple, and the altar, and those who worship in it. 2 Leave out the court which is outside of the temple, and don't measure it, for it has been given to the nations. <u>They will tread the holy city under foot for forty-two months.</u> 3 I will give power to my two witnesses, and they will prophesy one thousand two hundred sixty days, clothed in sackcloth."

As previously stated, the outline of Revelation dictates that the two parts of each of the two interludes have something in common with each other. The first part is the beginning of something and the second part is the end of the same thing. That makes the question; what is the angel with a scroll the beginning of, that makes the two witnesses the end of the same thing? The answer is, the message of the Gospel, the good news which gives condemned man a free opportunity to avoid the coming judgment. Jesus, the Lord, came to save men with this message He gave witness to. He was the beginning of announcing this opportunity to repent and be saved from that which has already been put into motion, and the two witnesses is the end of the announcing of that same opportunity.

However, there is a distinction between the message and audience the Lord speaks in the beginning, than that of the two witnesses. The two witnesses come 3-1/2 years before the Lord implements His decree of divorce (below):

NIV Rev 3:15 I know your deeds, that you are neither cold nor hot. I wish you were either one or the other!
NIV Rev 3:16 So, because you are lukewarm—neither hot nor cold—I am about to spit you out of my mouth.

"I am about to . . . " does not mean I am considering . . . Rather it means I have decided to spit you out of my mouth—I have decided to divorce you because of your spiritual adultery—I am going to:

NIV Mt 25:28 " <u>'Take the talent (the Holy Spirit) from him</u> and give it to the one who has the ten talents.

NIV Mt 25:29 *For everyone who has will be given more, and he will have an abundance.* <u>*Whoever*</u>
<u>*does not have, even what* (Holy Spirit) *he has will be taken from him.*</u>
NIV Mt 25:30 *And throw that worthless servant outside, into the darkness, where there will be*
weeping and gnashing of teeth.' (the great tribulation)

NIV Rev 3:17 *You say, 'I am rich; I have acquired wealth and do not need a thing.' But you do not*
realize that you are wretched, pitiful, poor, blind and naked.

However, as in the case of Hosea, Jesus uses the great tribulation to bring His people
back to their first love, and as such, makes a way, even at this point, to be reunited:

NIV Rev 3:18 <u>*I counsel you to buy from me gold refined in the fire*</u> (the great tribulation), *so*
you can become rich; and white clothes to wear (a celestial body), *so you can cover your*
shameful nakedness; and salve to put on your eyes, so you can see.
NIV Rev 3:19 *Those whom I love I rebuke and discipline. So be earnest, and repent.*

The two witnesses are not so much there for those who are blessed because they wait
and reach the end of the 1,335 days (Da 12:12) which is the *Church Pure* and the
rapture. They are primarily there for the *Church Corrupt* who are not caught up in
the rapture. They are there to speak the last words before Jesus vomits them out of
His mouth so that they know their hope is in buying gold refined in the fire—to
endure the great tribulation without coming off their testimony, without worshiping
the beast, or taking his mark, even to death. It says after the two witnesses are raised
up to heaven, the "rest" (those who remained) "were terrified, and gave glory to God
in heaven."

They were terrified and gave glory to God because through the profoundness of this
event they found out too late that the two witnesses were true and from God. It is
because of this happening; the two raising from the dead, then along with the Holy
Spirit and the *Church Pure* caught up to heaven and the earthquake, along with the
testimony of the two witnesses that they finally believed and their eyes were opened.
However, it was too late to have been included in what had just transpired. Their
only hope is to do as the two witnesses had told them to do: to not come off their
testimony of Christ, don't worship the beast, and do not take his mark, even to death.

The very hour they are finished with their 1,260 days of witnessing, they are killed, raised from the dead, and lifted up to heaven which marks the end and fulfillment of that witness to humanity that Jesus began. The end begins! The time of pardon is finished! Judgment begins first in the house of the Lord with 3-1/2 years of the great tribulation.

Amp Da 12:5 *Then I, Daniel, looked, and behold, there stood two others, the one on the brink of the river on this side and the other on the brink of the river on that side.*

Amp Da 12:6 *And one said to the man clothed in linen, who was above the waters of the river, How long shall it be to the end of these wonders?*

Amp Da 12:7 *And I heard the man clothed in linen, who was above the waters of the river, when he held up his right and his left hand toward the heavens and swore by Him Who lives forever that it shall be for a time, times, and a half a time [or three and one-half years]; and when they have made an end of shattering and crushing the power of the holy people, all these things shall be finished.*

The "shattering and crushing the power of the holy people" is the time of the great tribulation for 3-1/2 years. Then it ends with another 3-1/2 years of the wrath of God poured out on the world who persecuted them. However:

Amp 1Pe 4:17 *For the time [has arrived] for judgment to begin with the household of God; and if it begins with us, what will [be] the end of those who do not respect or believe or obey the good news (the Gospel) of God?*

Amp 1Pe 4:18 *And if the righteous are barely saved, what will become of the godless and wicked?*

The two witnesses are there as a final warning to endure the refining fire in a way to receive the gold. They are there because Jesus wanted clear that all is not lost and that, "*I advise you to buy from Me gold refined by fire . .*" They are not there so much as why Jesus was there in the first part to draw people into the Kingdom, but rather to draw those who fell away from the Kingdom by losing their first love. They are there so their hope is not lost but that when they wake up they are encouraged to finally do what is right. In doing so, the full number become His bride. Those who finally wake up are the great multitude. Paul tells us about that hour:

NAS 1TH 4:13 *But we do not want you to be uninformed, brethren, about those who are asleep, so that you will not grieve as do the rest who have no hope.*

NAS 1TH 4:14 *For if we believe that Jesus died and rose again, even so God will bring with Him those who have fallen asleep in Jesus.*

NAS 1TH 4:15 *For this we say to you by the word of the Lord, that we who are alive and remain until the coming of the Lord, will not precede those who have fallen asleep.*

NAS 1TH 4:16 *For the Lord Himself will descend from heaven with a shout, with the voice of the archangel and with the trumpet of God, and the dead in Christ will rise first* (the first resurrection).

NAS 1TH 4:17 *Then we who are alive and remain will be caught up together with them in the clouds to meet the Lord in the air, and so we shall always be with the Lord.*

The two witnesses are there to give hope to those who are followers of Christ who are a part of the *Church Corrupt.* Paul is not describing the rapture before the great tribulation. He is describing the "first resurrection" of the dead and the catching up into the sky to meet Jesus along with those who did not die, after the great tribulation. The reason there is a great multitude who did not come off their testimony of Christ, did not worship the beast or take his mark even at the cost of their lives is because the two witnesses were sent by Jesus to bring a close to what He Himself had begun. That is, Jesus knowing that some of His beloved would fail to make the mark, He still wanted to make a way for them.

Amp Ro 14:4 . . . *It is before his own master that he stands or falls. And he shall stand and be upheld, for the Master (the Lord) is mighty to support him and make him stand.*

Why put this second interlude here between the 6th and 7th trumpets?

Revelation makes note that after each of the first two woes the people know that all this comes from God. That is given the sky is opened up above them and they can see Him ready to come down. At the same time it was announced by God what will happen:

NIV Rev 8:13 *As I watched, I heard an eagle that was flying in midair call out in a loud voice: "Woe! Woe! Woe to the inhabitants of the earth, because of the trumpet blasts about to be sounded by the other three angels!"*

This is not some spiritual thing only heard by prophets. The heavens have opened up and all the earth sees and hears not only the trumpets sounding but this angelic creature announcing to the whole world the additional woes which will befall them. This eagle in the sky calling out in a loud voice is to the world what the two witnesses were to those Christians who had lost their first love. However, unlike the Christians who hang tight to their testimony even at the cost of their lives, the world does not heed, but instead continues to be hostile towards God. When it comes to the third and final woe, Jesus gives the world a final warning for their good, just as He had done for the elect through the two witnesses. Here is that warning:

NRSV Rev 16:12 The sixth angel poured his bowl on the great river Euphrates, and its water was dried up in order to prepare the way for the kings from the east. 13 And I saw three foul spirits like frogs coming from the mouth of the dragon, from the mouth of the beast, and from the mouth of the false prophet. 14 These are demonic spirits, performing signs, who go abroad to the kings of the whole world, to assemble them for battle on the great day of God the Almighty. 15 ("See, I am coming like a thief! Blessed is the one who stays awake and is clothed, not going about naked and exposed to shame.") 16 And they assembled them at the place that in Hebrew is called Harmagedon.

Verse 12 (above) is the second woe. This is in referring to the supernatural army of 200,000,000 being loosed and circling the globe while killing 1/3 of the world's population. Verses 13-16 (above) is what results in people preparing to meet their fate of the third woe, which is the battle of Armageddon. This battle will kill all who attend and oppose Christ out of their refusal to repent and reconcile with God—even to submit to His government He is about to impose on the earth. Thus the saying, "three strikes and you are out!" The world had three opportunities to have a change of heart as each succeeding opportunity exponentially worsened because of God's effort to show the world their futility of opposing Him. However, each woe points out that the people in the world refuse to repent of their crimes and put away their worship of false gods.

NIV Ps 2:1 Why do the nations conspire and the peoples plot in vain?
NIV Ps 2:2 The kings of the earth take their stand and the rulers gather together against the LORD and against his Anointed One.
NIV Ps 2:3 "Let us break their chains," they say, "and throw off their fetters."
NIV Ps 2:4 The One enthroned in heaven laughs; the Lord scoffs at them.
NIV Ps 2:5 Then he rebukes them in his anger and terrifies them in his wrath (the three woes), *saying,*

NIV Ps 2:6 "*I have installed my King on Zion, my holy hill.*"

At this point of what David is prophesying in Psalm 2 (above), "I have installed my King on Zion, my holy hill. . ." is between the sixth and seventh trumpet. It is the time when the mystery of God has been revealed. Jesus has come down from the sky and now resides in the supernatural city, the New Jerusalem; which comes down out of the spiritual realm to the natural earth. It is complete with its own mountain also made of supernatural matter (God's holy hill), leaving the world in total and utter darkness.

Inside the city is the wedding feast of the Lamb. All those who have become celestial humans are in attendance. Outside the city people are groping around in the darkness where there is weeping, and gnashing of teeth, people gnawing on their own tongues because of the overwhelmingness of their agony. The world and the government of the beast busies themselves recruiting and gathering their army to have the showdown of showdowns, a battle with the Lord who is now manifest on earth. The nations are bent on a fight to the death in order to prevent the Lord from ruling the world. They finally meet at Armageddon. David continues below to speak of his awe of their futileness.

NIV Ps 2:7 *I will proclaim the decree of the LORD: He said to me, "You are my Son; today I have become your Father.*
NIV Ps 2:8 *Ask of me, and I will make the nations your inheritance, the ends of the earth your possession.*
NIV Ps 2:9 *You will rule them with an iron scepter; you will dash them to pieces like pottery."*
NIV Ps 2:10 *Therefore, you kings, be wise; be warned, you rulers of the earth.*
NIV Ps 2:11 *Serve the LORD with fear and rejoice with trembling.*
NIV Ps 2:12 *Kiss the Son, lest he be angry and you be destroyed in your way, for his wrath can flare up in a moment. Blessed are all who take refuge in him.*

"See, I am coming like a thief! Blessed is the one who stays awake and is clothed, not going about naked and exposed to shame. And they assembled them at the place that in Hebrew is called Harmagedon." All throughout the Bible, God has referred to having a body as being clothed, and being a disembodied soul (dead) as being naked. This usage of being "clothed" is no more fitting than in this passage if one simply looks at the context of the rest of the verse. Jesus is not stopping in the middle of this important narrative to make a comment concerning a dress code. Jesus is warning the people not to be seduced by the demons in the mouths of the Devil, the beast, and the false prophet into joining those who will attempt to fight Him at the battle of Armageddon. By these words, Jesus is warning everyone that it will be plain suicide to do so. They will shamefully become disembodied souls—unclothed, shamefully naked. Why shamefully? Because as soon as that battle is finished Jesus will be the victor and a utopian peace and harmony will come upon the whole earth as a result of His rule. However, the dead will continue their torment. Torment they experienced having had endured the wrath of God for 3-1/2 years, and now because of their death at Armageddon resulting in their confinement in Hades, the realm of the dead.

The reason this second interlude was put here is because the Lord is showing every chance has been, and will be given to repent, right up until the end. He provides a way to avoid suffering the wrath and judgment of God. He has done His due diligence!

NIV 2Pe 3:7 By the same word the present heavens and earth are reserved for fire, being kept for the day of judgment and destruction of ungodly men.

NIV 2Pe 3:8 But do not forget this one thing, dear friends: With the Lord a day is like a thousand years, and a thousand years are like a day.

NIV 2Pe 3:9 The Lord is not slow in keeping his promise, as some understand slowness. He is patient with you, not wanting anyone to perish, but everyone to come to repentance.

NIV 2Pe 3:10 But the day of the Lord will come like a thief. The heavens will disappear with a roar; the elements will be destroyed by fire, and the earth and everything in it will be laid bare (naked—disembodied).

NIV 2Pe 3:11 Since everything will be destroyed in this way, what kind of people ought you to be? You ought to live holy and godly lives

NIV 2Pe 3:12 as you look forward to the day of God and speed its coming. That day will bring about the destruction of the heavens by fire, and the elements will melt in the heat.

NIV 2Pe 3:13 But in keeping with his promise we are looking forward to a new heaven and a new earth, the home of righteousness.

NIV 2Pe 3:14 So then, dear friends, since you are looking forward to this, make every effort to be found spotless, blameless and at peace with him.

WEB Rev 11:4 These (two witnesses) *are the two olive trees and the two lamp stands, standing before the Lord of the earth. 5 If anyone desires to harm them, fire proceeds out of their mouth and devours their enemies. If anyone desires to harm them, he must be killed in this way. 6 These have the power to shut up the sky, that it may not rain during the days of their prophecy. They have power over the waters, to turn them into blood, and to strike the earth with every plague, as often as they desire.*

"These (two witnesses) are the two olive trees and the two lamp stands, standing before the Lord of the earth." Who are these two and what is the significance of them being referred to as two olive trees, and two lampstands? Zechariah prophesied about these two witnesses. In Zechariah, Zerubbabel and Jeshua are the two olive trees and the two lamp stands. They were the local and contemporary fulfillment of the Zechariah prophecy. The two witnesses are the end times and global fulfillment of the two olive trees and the two lamp stands in his prophecy making it complete and accomplished. Let us look at what he said concerning the two olive trees and the two lampstands:

NIV Zec 4:7 "What are you, O mighty mountain? Before Zerubbabel you will become level ground. Then he will bring out the capstone to shouts of 'God bless it! God bless it!' "
NIV Zec 4:8 Then the word of the LORD came to me:
NIV Zec 4:9 "The hands of Zerubbabel have laid the foundation of this temple; his hands will also complete it. Then you will know that the LORD Almighty has sent me to you.

Zerubbabel and Jeshua who are accredited for the building of the second temple represent the local and contemporary manifestation of this prophecy by Zechariah. Jesus builds the next temple—the end times and global temples of God.

NIV 1Co 3:16 Don't you know that you yourselves are God's temple and that God's Spirit lives in you?
NIV 1Co 3:17 If anyone destroys God's temple, God will destroy him; for God's temple is sacred, and you are that temple.

However, Jesus does not build a stone temple as Zerubbabel and Jeshua had, He builds of living temples in the bodies of His followers who are in union with Him. By His hands Zerubbabel built the foundation and the altar of the temple and finishes it. By the words of Jesus, He built the foundation of His living temple in the hearts of

His followers and became the altar and sacrifice that finishes His living temples. He (Jesus) is the author and finisher of our faith (Hebrew 12:2).

NIV NIV Zec 4:10 *"Who despises the day of small things? Men will rejoice when they see the plumb line in the hand of Zerubbabel. "(These seven are the eyes of the LORD, which range throughout the earth.)"*

"These seven are the eyes of the LORD, which range throughout the earth." This is referring to when Jesus builds His living temples and His sevenfold Holy Spirit will reside in the hearts of those in union with Him. It represents the same as the Lamb with seven eyes John saw in the beginning of Revelation with His throat cut (sacrificed/slain).

Verse 10 (above) is referring to how the second temple was built in times of trouble and in a makeshift fashion, just as when Jesus made His living temples He was crucified before His message spread. Thus, who despises small beginnings?

NIV Zec 4:11 *Then I asked the angel, "What are these two olive trees on the right and the left of the lampstand?"*
NIV Zec 4:12 *Again I asked him, "What are these two olive branches beside the two gold pipes that pour out golden oil?"*
NIV Zec 4:13 *He replied, "Do you not know what these are?" "No, my lord," I said.*
NIV Zec 4:14 *So he said, "These are the two who are anointed to serve the Lord of all the earth."*

"When they see the plumb line in the hand of Zerubbabel . . ." This is prophetically speaking of when they see Jesus who has the ultimate plumb line and is the judge of what is true and right.

NIV Isa 28:16 *So this is what the Sovereign LORD says: "See, I lay a stone in Zion, a tested stone, a precious cornerstone for a sure foundation; the one who trusts will never be dismayed.*
NIV Isa 28:17 *I will make justice the measuring line and righteousness the plumb line; hail will sweep away your refuge, the lie, and water will overflow your hiding place.*
NIV Isa 28:18 *Your covenant with death will be annulled; your agreement with the grave will not stand.*

John had been given a rod, a measuring line of justice, a standard to measure or judge with.

NIV Eph 2:20 *built on the foundation of the apostles and prophets, with Christ Jesus himself as the chief cornerstone.*
NIV Eph 2:21 *In him the whole building is joined together and rises to become a holy temple in the Lord.*
NIV Eph 2:22 *And in him you too are being built together to become a dwelling in which God lives by his Spirit.*

God is building a living temple upon the foundation that the Apostles laid. The foundation is laid with their teachings and the integrity of the saints as the walls and Jesus as the chief cornerstone, which holds the whole building (the body) together.

NIV Rev 11:1 *I was given a reed like a measuring rod and was told, "Go and measure the temple of God and the altar, and count the worshipers there.*

The counting of the worshipers there inside the temple is another way of saying to qualify and quantify the *Church Pure* as being in union with Christ, according to the standard that John was given to measure with. Those who qualify will be raptured with the two witnesses. However, John is next told:

NIV Rev 11:2 *But exclude the outer court; do not measure it, because it has been given to the Gentiles. They will trample on the holy city for 42 months.*
NIV Rev 11:3 *And I will give power to my two witnesses, and they will prophesy for 1,260 days, clothed in sackcloth."*
NIV Rev 11:4 *These are the two olive trees and the two lampstands that stand before the Lord of the earth.*

John was told not to measure the outer court "for it has been given to the nations. They will trample on the holy city for forty-two months." 42 months are 3-1/2 years. This time period is the great tribulation. The trampling will be the killing of the *Church Corrupt*—the church left behind. The Christians in the outer court (as opposed to the ones inside the temple and at the altar) are representative of those who are neither hot nor cold, they are the ones Jesus divorces and spews out of His mouth. They are His Church but they are spiritually empowered by the beast and his Babylon (neither hot nor cold). They are the *Church Corrupt.* It is interesting that the word used is "trampled" (in most translations). Jesus once said:

NIV Mt 5:13 "You are the salt of the earth. But if the salt loses its saltiness, how can it be made salty again? It is no longer good for anything, <u>except to be thrown out and trampled by men.</u>

The trampling of the outer court are the killing of the Christians who don't measure up and are not counted to be among the worshipers in the temple—those caught up. However, as they are trampled by the nations, killed off, they become under the altar and are counted among the great multitude, who will be raised in the first resurrection. That is if they hang onto their testimony, do not worship the beast, or take his mark.

"I will give my two witnesses, and they will prophesy one thousand two hundred sixty days, clothed in sackcloth." It is important to take note that right after John is told that the outer court Christians are given up to be trampled on by the nations, the next verse immediately brings up the two witnesses. Although the two witnesses have been raptured before the trampling begins, speaking of them at this point is most significant. That reason is because it is what they had testified to when they were being rejected. Now that what they said comes true, those who would not listen or believe them sober up. Those who believed too late are left to endure the great tribulation, however, they now will stay true to their testimony, not worship the beast, or take his mark, and thereby be resurrected and saved.

It is the witness of these two which ensures there are countless many who will be a part of the first resurrection. They will join the survivors by being lifted up into the sky, while receiving their celestial bodies, and taking their place as the bride. Because of their witness the great multitude fulfills the numbers needed to add to the 144,000 that finally starts the wrath of God coming down on the world.

If their testimony had not been enough to ensure that those who did not believe them would when the great tribulation comes, the circumstances surrounding the death and resurrection of the two witnesses will. When their 3-1/2 years of testifying finishes, the Lord has it within His power to bring them up to heaven any way He wishes. So then, the question is, why let them suffer being murdered by the risen beast? The Lord causes them to suffer death because it makes their testimony complete. They have been telling those who do not believe that when everything that they told them happens and the great tribulation comes and they finally believe, they should remember what they preached. That is, do not come off your testimony of Christ, do not worship the beast, and do not take his mark even under the pain of death, then they will be saved and rise from their death.

The two witnesses die because the risen beast kills them. All those who do not deny Christ, worship the beast, and take his mark will also be killed by the beast or his agents just as the two witnesses were. Then, according to what they preached, the two witnesses raise back to life 3-1/2 days later, representing the 3-1/2 years later at the end of the great tribulation when those who died in it are raised back to life. Afterwards they are lifted up to join Jesus in the sky. This is the exact thing the two witnesses will be telling the people who doubt and are left behind that will happen to them if they do not deny their testimony in Christ. When those left behind realize they were foolish, and see what happens to the two witnesses was exactly what they said would happen, they will make up their resolve to not pass up their last chance. They will now know that what happened to the two witnesses will happen to them, they too will rise up to everlasting life, just as the two witnesses did. It will be their only hope and confidence!

Note: It is in the same way that Jesus proved His testimony as true by raising from death after three days in the grave. Zerubbabel and Jeshua by their hands built the stone temple, however, in Zechariah a word was given to Zerubbabel who typified Christ:

NIV Zec 4:6 So he said to me, "This is the word of the LORD to Zerubbabel: 'Not by might nor by power, but by my Spirit,' says the LORD Almighty.
NIV Zec 4:7 "What are you, O mighty mountain? Before Zerubbabel you will become level ground. Then he will bring out the capstone to shouts of 'God bless it! God bless it!' "

It is the same for those who hold to their testimony and are rescued from among the dead at the first resurrection, 3-1/2 years after the beginning of the great tribulation. It is by the power of the Holy Spirit that they are rescued from the grave and are resurrected as Jesus was and the two witnesses will be.

The two witnesses not only set the standard by which those in the great tribulation can still be saved, but they demonstrate it. Those left behind can see the testimony of the two witnesses is true because they were killed like Jesus, yet lived. The *Church Corrupt* sees that even if they themselves are killed, they know proof positive that they too will rise, live, and be brought to Jesus. Yes, the two witnesses are the end of what Jesus began!

> WEB Rev 11:7 *When they have finished their testimony, the beast that comes up out of the abyss will make war with them, and overcome them, and kill them.*

The beast will come up out from among the dead and have his 42 months because he has at heart to break the power of the holy people. He starts by killing the two witnesses.

> WEB Rev 11:8 *Their dead bodies will be in the street of the great city, which spiritually is called Sodom and Egypt, where also their Lord was crucified. 9 From among the peoples, tribes, languages, and nations people will look at their dead bodies for three and a half days, and will not allow their dead bodies to be laid in a tomb. 10 Those who dwell on the earth rejoice over them, and they will be glad. They will give gifts to one another, because these two prophets tormented those who dwell on the earth. 11 After the three and a half days, the breath of life from God entered into them, and they stood on their feet. Great fear fell on those who saw them. 12 I heard a loud voice from heaven saying to them, "Come up here!" They went up into heaven in the cloud, and their enemies saw them*

The same thing that happens to them will happen to the great multitude at the end of the 3-1/2 years (3-1/2 days) they (the two olive trees) have laid the foundation and the altar for those who will be persecuted. They have shown the way.

> . 13 In that day there was a great earthquake (the same earthquake as in Rev: 6:12), *and a tenth of the city fell. Seven thousand people were killed in the earthquake, and the rest were terrified, and gave glory to the God of heaven.*

The Holy Spirit, the two witnesses, and the *Church Pure* leave the earth for 42 months. The great tribulation begins.

> WEB Rev 11:14 *The second woe is past. Behold, the third woe comes quickly.*

This verse (above) signals the end of this second interlude. It is a segue to transition back to the trumpets. We pick up where things were left off, that is somewhere between the sixth and seventh trumpet blast.

The Second Interlude Ends

and

the Narrative of the Trumpets Resume

The second woe was the release of the supernatural army of 200,000,000 that circled the globe and killed 1/3 of mankind to get justice for the 1/3 of the saints who were killed during the first 3-1/2 years. That second woe had followed after the first which was the stinging scorpion like supernatural creatures which also came out of the Abyss. It is not clear whether the agony of their stings will last 5 months with each sting, or that the creatures are manifest for 5 months plaguing the people at will with their stings. Nevertheless, the first two woes come in a way which comprise almost the entire 3-1/2 years of the wrath of God.

However, even if there is a break between these two woes, the Devil, his angels, and (God knows what) other supernatural creatures who escaped the Abyss are on the earth manifest, hostile and dominating towards humans. Likewise, those 2 woes happen with a backdrop of natural disasters and catastrophic events which make life all but unlivable as well as provisions and shelter made scarce, and eventual contamination of all the drinking water or it has turned to blood. The cities are leveled by earthquakes and fires, the infrastructure of utilities and energy destroyed, and the highways broken apart. The earth is pummeled with meteors. John takes note that one of them is like the size of a mountain top which devastates the oceans and throws off the entire ecosystem as it comes down like a big fireball. It will be a time of dog-eat-dog. It will not only be humans who are desperate for survival, but the animal kingdom as well.

It is not revealed exactly when it is no longer a third of the sky from horizon to horizon which views the spiritual realm, and when the earth is fully pushed into it resulting in total and utter darkness 24 hours a day. However, it has been decreed to happen. There will be no heavenly bodies to give off light when that occurs. Although the darkness will bring an end to the scorching heat and destroying fires which burn all over the earth as a result of the rolling up of the sky that closes the distance to the sun, does it really bring relief? How will plants grow? Jesus says it will be so dark and people will be in so much distress that they will gnaw at their own tongues.

NIV Rev 10:7 But in the days when the seventh angel is about to sound his trumpet, the mystery of God will be accomplished, just as he announced to his servants the prophets."

After the second woe has done its work and the 3-1/2 years is just about concluded, the sight the world sees up in the sky comes down to the earth. These days when the seventh angel is about to sound his trumpet, is when so much of God's plan for judgment, salvation, and how He is going to make His dwelling place among men will have happened. The mysteries of God will then have been accomplished. In other words, it is before this seventh trumpet that after the sky had rolled open, the Lord, His angels, His elect in their glorified bodies, and the New Jerusalem have come down to the earth, as a part of His second coming.

The first resurrection will have happened before Jesus touches down with His entourage and supernatural city. People were terrified when the two witnesses came back to life. Like the two witnesses there will be a time between when they rise back to life and when they are called up into the sky with those who survived to line up behind Jesus and follow Him in His descent. The people of the world will be absolutely mortified—paralyzed in fear when the billions of people they killed suddenly rise back up to life and walk the earth again. Between the dead rising, the sight of Jesus in the sky ready to come down and carry out justice, and supernatural creatures haunting them, the people of the world will look for holes in the ground to crawl in, as they grope around in total darkness trying to survive.

While the celestial humans are on earth enjoying the wedding feast inside the walls of the New Jerusalem, outside will no longer have even the light of the image of Jesus in the sky ready to come down. When Jesus tells His parables about that return or about that wedding feast, He makes note of those who were not worthy to be a part of it and inside the walls of the city. First of all, the city is made in heaven, and therefore constructed of spiritual matter and not natural matter. Secondly, Jesus makes it clear that natural flesh cannot enter into the city. They must be a celestial human possessing wedding clothes—a celestial body to enter in. In these parables He ends them all with the same conclusion, that those who do not qualify to become a celestial human will have to suffer being outside the walls. Where Jesus describes in the verses below:

NIV Lk 13:23 Someone asked him, "Lord, are only a few people going to be saved?" He said to them,

NIV Lk 13:24 "Make every effort to enter through the narrow door, because many, I tell you, will try to enter and will not be able to.

NIV Lk 13:25 Once the owner of the house gets up and closes the door, you will stand outside knocking and pleading, 'Sir, open the door for us.' "But he will answer, 'I don't know you or where you come from.'

NIV Lk 13:26 "Then you will say, 'We ate and drank with you, and you taught in our streets.'

NIV Lk 13:27 "But he will reply, 'I don't know you or where you come from. Away from me, all you evildoers!'

NIV Lk 13:28 "There will be weeping there, and gnashing of teeth, when you see Abraham, Isaac and Jacob and all the prophets in the kingdom of God, but you yourselves thrown out.

NIV Lk 13:29 People will come from east and west and north and south, and will take their places at the feast in the kingdom of God.

NIV Lk 13:30 Indeed there are those who are last who will be first, and first who will be last."

====================

NIV Mt 8:10 When Jesus heard this, he was astonished and said to those following him, "I tell you the truth, I have not found anyone in Israel with such great faith.

NIV Mt 8:11 I say to you that many will come from the east and the west, and will take their places at the feast with Abraham, Isaac and Jacob in the kingdom of heaven.

NIV Mt 8:12 But the subjects of the kingdom will be thrown outside, into the darkness, where there will be weeping and gnashing of teeth."

NIV Mt 8:13 Then Jesus said to the centurion, "Go! It will be done just as you believed it would."

====================

NIV Mt 24:47 I tell you the truth, he will put him in charge of all his possessions.

NIV Mt 24:48 But suppose that servant is wicked and says to himself, 'My master is staying away a long time,'

NIV Mt 24:49 and he then begins to beat his fellow servants and to eat and drink with drunkards.

NIV Mt 24:50 The master of that servant will come on a day when he does not expect him and at an hour he is not aware of.

NIV Mt 24:51 He will cut him to pieces and assign him a place with the hypocrites, where there will be weeping and gnashing of teeth.

====================

NIV Mt 25:10 "But while they were on their way to buy the oil, the bridegroom arrived. The virgins who were ready went in with him to the wedding banquet. And the door was shut.

NIV Mt 25:11 "Later the others also came. 'Sir! Sir!' they said. 'Open the door for us!'

NIV Mt 25:12 "But he replied, 'I tell you the truth, I don't know you.'

====================

NIV Mt 25:28 " 'Take the talent from him and give it to the one who has the ten talents.

NIV Mt 25:29 For everyone who has will be given more, and he will have an abundance. Whoever does not have, even what he has will be taken from him.

NIV Mt 25:30 And throw that worthless servant outside, into the darkness, where there will be weeping and gnashing of teeth.'

The seventh trumpet

WEB Rev 11:15 The seventh angel sounded, and great voices in heaven followed, saying, "The kingdom of the world has become the Kingdom of our Lord, and of his Christ. He will reign forever and ever!" 16 The twenty-four elders, who sit on their thrones before God's throne, fell on their faces and worshiped God, 17 saying: "We give you thanks, Lord God, the Almighty, the one who is and who was; because you have taken your great power, and reigned.

The third and final woe is the release of demons who, through the beast, the false prophet and the manifest Devil himself, seduce the people of the world into gathering and rising up to fight Jesus' arrival on the earth. The result is all who gather, die.

These verses (above) signify that Jesus has come out from behind the walls of the New Jerusalem to conquer all in the world who would oppose His rule to take over the whole earth. It is the time of the great supper when the scavenger birds will gorge themselves on the flesh of the dead.

This is so ironic. It is like the head and tails of the same coin. The coin is a feast. Heads is the wedding feast of the Lamb inside the walls of the New Jerusalem. The tails of the same coin is the great supper of the Lord, when every type of scavenger bird that exists will feed on the countless bodies of those who died opposing Christ in the battle of Armageddon (the third woe).

The battle of Armageddon has transpired, and Jesus has emerged as the victor. He will call His people, the Israelites, back to their land in Israel. The nations will bow down to Jesus and line up under His rule serving the Israelites and their King for a thousand years. The light which spills out from inside the New Jerusalem will be the light which illuminates the earth, for there will be no sun or moon or stars.

Amp Zec 14:1 *BEHOLD, A day of the Lord is coming when the spoil [taken from you] shall be divided [among the victors] in the midst of you.*
Amp Zec 14:2 *For I will gather all nations against Jerusalem to battle, and the city shall be taken and the houses rifled and the women ravished; and half of the city shall go into exile, but the rest of the people shall not be cut off from the city.*

The above verses are talking about the 42 months of the beast, during the great tribulation.

Amp Zec 14:3 *Then shall the Lord go forth and fight against those nations, as when He fought in the day of battle.*

Verse 3 (above) is reference to the battle of Armageddon

Amp Zec 14:4 *And His feet shall stand in that day upon the Mount of Olives, which lies before Jerusalem on the east, and the Mount of Olives shall be split in two from the east to the west by a very great valley; and half of the mountain shall remove toward the north and half of it toward the south.*

Amp Zec 14:5 *And you shall flee by the valley of My mountains, for the valley of the mountains shall reach to Azal, and you shall flee as you fled from before the earthquake in the days of Uzziah king of Judah; and the Lord my [Zechariah's] God shall come, and all the holy ones [saints and angels] with Him.*

Verses 4 and 5 (above) digresses a bit from the conclusion and summary of verses 1-3 (above). It backs up to give details of Jesus' return and conquering takeover of the world government. When He touches down on the Mount of Olives there is an earthquake which when splits creates a huge east to west running valley. The people of the world who resided in the great city of Babylon, which is at this time during the reign of the beast, Jerusalem, will flee for their lives using this new valley created by this tremendous earthquake.

Not only Jesus has touched down causing this shift in the topography of the region, but a mountain from the spiritual realm of which on the top of it is a city that follows down behind Jesus. A city that is approximately 80% of the size of the mainland of the United States. That is along with His Father, His army angels, and the countless celestial humans all of which will reside in this supernatural city/state. You can be assured in their panic they will flee like cockroaches in an infested kitchen when the lights go on, at the advent of this moment and the massive mountain coming down filled with light and splendor contrasting the complete and utter darkness.

Amp Zec 14:6 *And it shall come to pass in that day that there shall not be light; the glorious and bright ones [the heavenly bodies] shall be darkened.*
Amp Zec 14:7 *But it shall be one continuous day, known to the Lord—not day and not night, but at evening time there shall be light.*
Amp Zec 14:8 *And it shall be in that day that living waters shall go out from Jerusalem, half of them to the eastern [Dead] Sea and half of them to the western [Mediterranean] Sea; in summer and in winter shall it be.*
Amp Zec 14:9 *And the Lord shall be King over all the earth; in that day the Lord shall be one [in the recognition and worship of men] and His name one.*
Amp Zec 14:10 *All the land shall be turned into a plain from Geba to Rimmon, [the Rimmon that is] south of Jerusalem. But Jerusalem shall remain lifted up on its site and dwell in its place, from Benjamin's gate to the place of the First Gate, to the Corner Gate, and from the Tower of Hananel to the king's winepresses.*

Amp Zec 14:11 *And it shall be inhabited, for there shall be no more curse or ban of utter destruction, but Jerusalem shall dwell securely.*

Amp Zec 14:12 <u>*And this shall be the plague wherewith the Lord will smite all the peoples that have warred against Jerusalem: their flesh shall rot away while they stand upon their feet and their eyes shall corrode away in their sockets and their tongue shall decay away in their mouth.*</u>

This is what will happen at Armageddon when by the sword (words) that come out of Jesus' mouth and kill every single person there arrayed against Him. That is with the exception of the beast and false prophet who already had lived once and as such will be cast alive into the lake of fire, being its first recipients. Lastly, the Devil will be chained and thrown in the Abyss of the realm of the dead to be confined until that day he will be loosed on the earth a final time with Gog and Magog. After that battle, he will come to his final destination, the lake of fire.

Amp Zec 14:13 <u>*And in that day there shall be a great confusion, discomfiture, and panic among them from the Lord; and they shall seize each his neighbor's hand, and the hand of the one shall be raised against the hand of the other.*</u>

Amp Zec 14:14 *And Judah also shall fight at Jerusalem, and the wealth of all the nations round about shall be gathered together—gold and silver and apparel in great abundance.*

Amp Zec 14:15 *And as that plague on men, so shall be the plague on the horse, on the mule, on the camel, on the donkey, and on all the livestock and beasts that may be in those camps.*

After the confusion of the aftermath of that battle, the Lord will establish His 1,000 year reign. It is then that the healing of the earth and the curse of the four horsemen will be lifted.

Amp Zec 14:16 *And everyone who is left of all the nations which came against Jerusalem shall even go up from year to year to worship the King, the Lord of hosts, and to keep the Feast of Tabernacles or Booths.*

The nations will be healed by the ministering celestial humans and angels. However, the nations will be forced to take their place as subordinate to those who they hated, the Jews and Israelites. If they resist in serving them, the verses below describe the consequences. It is because of the malcontent of the populations of the nations outside of Israel who are still divided in their hearts when it comes to yielding to the Lord, that it will necessitate one last conflict. This conflict will expose all who would choose rebellion against the Lord. That conflict is those who would gather to fight the Lord with the Devil and Gog and Magog 1,000 years later, soon before the last day of the natural earth's existence.

Amp Zec 14:17 *And it shall be that whoso of the families of the earth shall not go up to Jerusalem to worship the King, the Lord of hosts, upon them there shall be no rain.*
Amp Zec 14:18 *And if the family of Egypt does not go up to Jerusalem and present themselves, upon them there shall be no rain, but there shall be the plague with which the Lord will smite the nations that go not up to keep the Feast of Tabernacles.*
Amp Zec 14:19 *This shall be the consequent punishment of the sin of Egypt and the consequent punishment of the sin of all the nations that do not go up to keep the Feast of Tabernacles.*

However, the Lord's people, the natural humans who comprise Israel will live in bliss. It will be a utopian existence with the curses lifted which oppressed mankind since soon after the flood—the first four seals, the four horsemen which are the four winds of God's destruction.

Amp Zec 14:20 *In that day there shall be [written] upon the [little] bells on the horses, HOLY TO THE LORD, and the pots in the Lord's house shall be holy to the Lord like the bowls before the altar.*
Amp Zec 14:21 *Yes, every pot in all the houses of Jerusalem and in Judah shall be dedicated and holy to the Lord of hosts, and all who sacrifice may come and take of them and boil their sacrifices in them [and traders in such wares will no longer be seen at the temple]. And in that day there shall be no more a Canaanite [that is, any godless or unclean person, whether Jew or Gentile] in the house of the Lord of hosts.*

> *WEB Rev 11:18a* *The nations were angry, and your wrath came, as did the time for the dead to be judged, . . .*

These final two verses concluding the seven trumpets and the seven seals they are a part of, speak of the conclusion of God's plan of judgment and salvation as it carefully complies with His promise to Noah. This has to be included because the seven seals reveal the sevenness of God's plan of judgment and redemption for the world. It is speaking of the last day when the earth will be destroyed. With a thunderous crash all the elements of nature will melt in the fire and all the natural or mortal humans will in an instant become disembodied/dead. No trace of the earth, and all natural humans are extinct, as has been planned by God. Those who suddenly find themselves bodiless with no earth below their feet, will join those who from the beginning of humanity have died and are likewise bodiless held confined in Hades. Together they will be resurrected and be given a body by which to face the throne of God for judgment.

Death entered into the world because of the sin of Adam and Eve, however, now every single person who ever lived and died will once again be alive clothed in a body. The realm of the dead, Hades, will have been emptied, no longer needed to temporarily confine the disembodied souls of the dead. It will therefore be cast into the lake of fire where the earth had just disappeared into.

As they stand before the seat of judgment they will now be judged fairly not by the folly of Adam, but by how they conducted themselves in the body. If they, by their own evil, are found unacceptable, they will be cast alive to suffer a second but permanent death in the lake of fire and will be in torment for eternity.

If, however, they are found acceptable in how they conducted themselves when alive in the body, they will be declared approved, given a celestial body and become citizens in the new heavens and new earth. However, they will never hold the status of "bride" who already had become celestial humans and did not face judgment or the lake of fire. The bride, many of whom never even tasted death but were transformed into their celestial bodies before their heart stopped beating, will be the government in the new heavens and the new earth for all of eternity. In fact, they will sit in chairs to judge and witness on the last day when the rest of the world is judged.

The seventh trumpet and seal concludes with mention of this closure of mankind, the earth and the universe it dwelled in.

> *WEB Rev 11:18b* ... *and to give your bondservants the prophets, their reward, as well as to the saints, and those who fear your name, to the small and the great; and to destroy those who destroy the earth."*

This brings a conclusion to the sevenness of God's plan for final judgment and salvation as told through the first of the four narratives of Revelation called, "The Seven Seals."

Bibliography

Amplified Bible. Scripture quotations marked (Amp) are taken from the Amplified Bible, Copyright © 1954, 1958, 1962, 1964, 1965, 1987 by The Lockman Foundation. Used by permission.

Gisborn, T. (n.d.). *Nimrod the Worlds First Tyrant and Forerunner of the Antichrist.* Retrieved October 2012, from Hubpages: http://eliora.hubpages.com/hub/NIMROD-THE-WORLDS-FIRST-TYRANT-AND-FORERUNNER-OF-THE-ANTICHRIST

Good News Translation (Today's English Version, Second Edition). Scripture quotations marked (GNT) are from the Good News Translation in Today's English Version- Second Edition, Copyright © 1992 by American Bible Society. Used by Permission.

(n.d.). Kitāb Al-Magāll or The Book of the Rolls. In One of the Books of Clement. Retrieved from http://www.sacred-texts.com/chr/aa/aa2.htm

New American Standard. Scripture quotations marked (NAS) are taken from the NEW AMERICAN STANDARD BIBLE®, Copyright © 1960,1962,1963,1968,1971,1972,1973,1975,1977,1995 by The Lockman Foundation. Used by permission.

New International Version. Scriptures taken from the Holy Bible, New International Version®, NIV®. Copyright © 1973, 1978, 1984 by Biblica, Inc.™ Used by permission of Zondervan. All rights reserved worldwide. www.zondervan.com The "NIV" and "New International Version" are trademarks registered in the United States Patent and Trademark Office by Biblica, Inc.™

New Living Translation. Holy Bible, New Living Translation copyright © 1996, 2004, 2007 by Tyndale House Foundation. Used by permission of Tyndale House Publishers Inc., Carol Stream, Illinois 60188. All rights reserved. New Living, NLT, and the New Living Translation logo are registered` trademarks of Tyndale House Publishers.

New Revised Standard Version Bible (NRSV), copyright © 1989 National Council of the Churches of Christ in the United States of America. Used by permission. All rights reserved worldwide.

Nimrod. (2013, December 3). Retrieved October 2012, from Wikipedia, The Free Encyclopedia: http://en.wikipedia.org/wiki/Nimrod

World English Bible. Scripture quotations marked (WEB) are taken from The World English Bible, which is in the public domain. Special thanks to Michael Paul Johnson and all who worked on the translation as a means to release a modern version of the Bible that is available for non-copyright use. A reminder that the Bible is not owned by man.

ABOUT THE AUTHORS

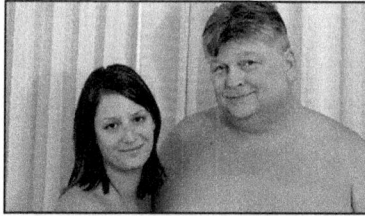

We are just a voice

WEB Jn 1:19 This is John's testimony (about himself), *when the Jews sent priests and Levites from Jerusalem to ask him, "Who are you?"*
WEB Jn 1:20 He declared, and didn't deny, but he declared, "I am not the Christ."
WEB Jn 1:21 They asked him, "What then? Are you Elijah?"
He said, "I am not."
"Are you the prophet?"
He answered, "No."
WEB Jn 1:22 They said therefore to him, "Who are you? Give us an answer to take back to those who sent us. What do you say about yourself?"
WEB Jn 1:23 He said, "__I am the voice__ of one crying in the wilderness, 'Make straight the way of the Lord ..'"

True prophets in the Bible did not convince people who they were; in fact, they refused to talk about themselves. They refused to bring credibility to the words of God they spoke by trying to get people to believe who they were and trust them. They knew that it would be profaning the words of God to do so, and it would be elevating themselves above God's words. They knew that God's words have their own credibility because they are from God. And God will show them (His own words) as from Him.

God's prophets also knew that those who truly love God will, therefore, benefit from their words, and those who are lovers of themselves will not benefit from them, because they will be dismissive and not trust them. The time is over that we look at the person who speaks to decide if we believe. We must begin to discern if the words are from God and if they carry God's Spirit.

You might say to that, "but not everyone can discern God." If that is the case, then they indict themselves as not being "known" by Jesus. They unwittingly reveal about themselves that they desire to do their own will and not the Lord's, just as the religious leaders who wanted Jesus to prove His credibility so they could decide if His words were from God.

Amp Jn 7:16 Jesus answered them by saying, My teaching is not My own, but His Who sent Me. Amp Jn 7:17 If any man desires to do His will (God's pleasure), he will know (have the needed illumination to recognize, and can tell for himself) whether the teaching is from God or whether I am speaking from Myself and of My own accord and on My own authority.

Many will think this is an oversimplified notion. However, it is so simple that it is not only true but reveals a simple but foundational truth about the person. What Jesus is saying is that if a man has a pure heart and wants to do the will of God above his own will, then what seems intuitively right (what sets well with that man) will be God's will and His words. However, even if you are a scholar, theologian, or work in the field of religion, and you desire to carry out your own will, having your own agendas and ambitions, well then, what seems right to that man is not God's will or His words, but that which lines up with his own will.

Generally speaking, the greatest religious minds in the world judge if something is from God by looking at the standing and qualifications of the man speaking them. In the above case, Jesus shows they may be smart in their own eyes, believing they know what is from God and therefore able to judge according to their knowledge of God. However, that would be saying in effect, we know everything about God because of our great knowledge. Therefore, if you say anything outside of our knowledge of God, or outside of the knowledge base of the accepted theological models, or if you are not a qualified student of those accepted models, then we must deduce your words are not from God.

To Jesus, they show about themselves that they don't recognize His words as from God because of their personal acquaintance with God. Instead, they have to judge by facts. They show themselves as having no real relationship with God; they would not recognize Him when He stands right before them. As a matter of fact, on another occasion when they showed contempt for Him, Jesus said of them:

NIV Jn 5:42 ... but I know you. I know that you do not have the love of God in your hearts.

They were once again wanting Him to prove who He was, and what right He had to talk the way He did. Jesus, instead of being intimidated, marveled at how He spoke and acted out everything the Father willed, yet they did not recognize His words as His Father's. Furthermore, they were, by nature, hostile and offended towards those words.

Let's look at that closer through an illustration. For example, you have a woman who claims to be married to a man named Jim. Then, a man claiming to be Jim and her husband approaches her. The above case is like the wife doubting this man is her husband. So then, she begins to question him. For example, "If you're Jim, when were you born?" And, "What kind of car did you have when you first got your license?" If he doesn't answer to her satisfaction, she decides that he is not her husband Jim. This might seem reasonable, and if he got the answers incorrect or didn't remember, the people listening might believe her when she says, "this is not my husband."

If there was anybody in the crowd that had wisdom, they might say this begs another question, "Hey lady, are you really Jim's wife or are you an imposter?" The reasoning of the wise man is, do you really need factual evidence to know if he is your husband? Don't you know your husband when he is standing right in front of you? Jesus is marveling at the religious leaders who are supposed to know God and claim to be in union with Him. However, they don't recognize Him when He stands before them. They don't even recognize His words as from God. Do they really need factual evidence to know something that they are supposed to have intimate knowledge of? Next question, why does it not occur to anyone to question if these men of God, leaders of the Jewish faith, may be imposters because they don't judge if someone and their words are from God by their intimate knowledge of God? They need factual evidence?

What did that tell Jesus? It told Him that even the top religious leaders who know the written word by heart can't recognize God when they stand right in front of Him.

It told Him that they were, in their inner man, hostile and threatened by God's words. It told Him that, in their inner selves, they really had no love or even any natural attraction towards God, His heart, and the Spirit of His words. They were obviously naturally repelled by them; they had no real love for God and their response showed it. However, to the religious leaders, they thought themselves wise and discerning to hold Jesus and His words suspect by judging Him with factual evidence. How disappointing it must have been to Jesus that the best of the best had no intimate knowledge of God and they were repulsed by Him when facing Him. Yes, Jesus' deduction was correct, there was no love of God in their hearts.

It is a Biblical fact that the major way we will be judged is it will be proven if we have a natural attraction to please God and do His will, therefore saying about us that we love Him more than ourselves. Learning by the folly of the leaders and the scholarly of Jesus' day, it is not by a knowledgeable and scholarly mind that one can successfully judge or discern what words coming from what person are from God or not. You can't judge superficially. No, it takes something much greater than to know every Bible verse by heart and to be able to have insightful knowledge of the person speaking them. It actually takes something much harder to attain than perfect scholarly knowledge of the written word. It takes a pure heart. Not meaning a sinless heart, but one which is single-minded, wanting to please God by serving Him and wanting to do His will at the expense of their own. This is what qualifies one to recognize if something is from God.

WEB Mt 5:8 *Blessed are the pure in heart, for they shall see God.*

It is true that as Colleen and I gain a larger following of our teachings and ministry, people will undoubtedly come to know us personally, and what kind of people we are. However, as teachers, we teach people how to live as spiritual men and women, discerning life in a spiritual way.

We have found the best way to teach discerning of spirit. It is not by knowing how to figure people out or to train them to have a spiritual power. No, we teach them to be single-minded when it comes to God, to be surrendered to His will in a pure or holistic way.

Having a still spirit which is not agitated with passions will create a huge contrast. The contrast of having the stillness of God's Spirit rule your heart coming in contact with the agitated spirit energies the people of this world operate out of makes one sensitive to discern spirit.

Jesus was right; wanting to do God's will with all your heart alone will cause you to recognize if one has God's Spirit in them and if they speak word's which are from God. As the saying goes, "You can't cheat an honest man."

NIV Jn 8:15 You judge by human standards. . .

NIV Jn 7:24 Stop judging by mere appearances, and make a right judgment."

As such, Colleen and I would like to be known first as a voice, just a voice. We want the words we speak from God to have more prominence and have their own credibility, than that of who we are. Therefore, we don't want to propagate people judging superficially if one is from God by giving our Bio. We want the words we speak to be more important than who we are. We want those who have a pure heart in wanting to serve God to check in their heart if we and the words we speak are from God.

We want those who don't have a pure heart to have a change of heart so they may know for themselves the voice and words of God when they hear them. However, we want to point people in the way to properly discern so they may know for themselves if we are from God and speak His words; in the same way John the Baptist tried to convey. You ask about us, and we will tell you about Him. You insist on wanting to know about us, and we will then tell you, we are just a voice making way for the One you should know and should be asking about. We are not a face or a name or people you should want to know, we are just a voice which gives voice to the One whose words you need to know.

OTHER BOOKS BY THE NAKED APOSTLES

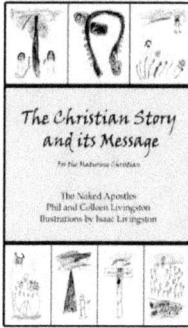

The Christian Story
and its Message

Christianity:
A Lost Civilization

For ordering information please visit our website at
www.nakedapostles.org

OTHER BOOKS BY THE NAKED APOSTLES

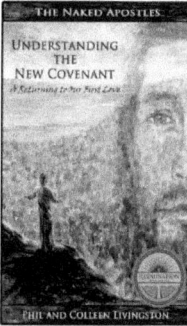

Understanding
the
New Covenant:
*A Returning to Our
First Love*

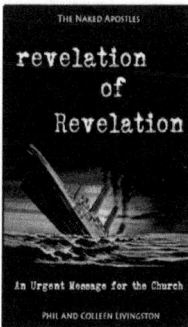

revelation of Revelation:
*An Urgent Message
for the Church*

Volumes 1-6

For ordering information please visit our website at
www.nakedapostles.org